Tony

To our man!

Enjoy the VF-22

[signature]

PRAISE FOR *DIVERSITY AND INCLUSION THE SUBMARINE WAY*

Of all the pivotal influences I encountered in the military, John Vincent was the one who ignited the fire of my military career. I served with John when he was chief of the boat onboard the USS *Pennsylvania*. I was a 23-year-old sailor with my mind set on getting out at the end of my contract; until I met John. From day one, there was a distinct difference onboard the *Pennsylvania*. His leadership and vision was the vehicle of a huge cultural shift that took place. As a different leader than any other I had served with, rather than *having* to follow him, I *wanted* to follow him. As an engaged leader, he was confident, poised, and had a strong presence. His style of inclusion, the value he placed on sailors and the team, coupled with his emotional intellect, created and sustained an environment where sailors naturally and continually excelled. My tour on the *Pennsylvania* was one of the defining moments in my life. Unsure of what I wanted to do in life, my time onboard with John sharpened my goals and set me out on a journey. Not only did I continue my service, because of his example, I gained a passion for and pursued leadership. With twenty-four years of service and counting, I'm now on my fourth tour as a command master chief. I constantly reflect on his examples of leadership during my time on the *Pennsylvania* and strive to incorporate them at each command. I wouldn't be where I am today without the leadership lessons and inspiration of John Vincent.

CMDCM(AW/SS) J. R. Consford

Command Master Chief
VAQ-129 Vikings

Diversity and Inclusion The Submarine Way was both insightful and revealing. Deb and John write about two seemingly disparate and unrelated environments: the close confines of a submarine juxtaposed against the similarly close quarters of the business boardroom. John's incredible stories of life on a submarine as well as the processes and techniques that induce high performance levels should serve as a reminder to all of the unlimited potential that can released by a diverse and inclusive workforce. As one of Deb's colleagues, I also witnessed how a diverse and inclusive environment induced high performance teams to achieve the seemingly impossible, not once but multiple times. I commend Deb and John for demonstrating how successful processes and techniques employed beneath the waves can generate similar results in the business world.

Carey Mason

CEO
The Alternative Board

This is brilliant. We must look beyond affirmative action, which was groundbreaking and critical in its time, and look to the future. As Deb and John so effectively put it, the survival of mankind depends on the concept of inclusion.

Pat Stowers

Operations Manager
Infosys McCamish Systems, LLC

What John and Deb have put together in *The Submarine Way* is nothing short of astonishing. They have managed to put lessons and insights it would take most of us a lifetime to learn into a few chapters. Their work is inspiring, thoughtful and, amazingly accessible. Follow their lead and success is virtually certain.

George Reynolds

Manager,
Travelers Human Resources,

Captivating and transformative … This book masterfully illustrates core principles for diversity and inclusion and provides takeaways for business and life. It's filled with conviction, passion, and excellent storytelling. A must read for anyone.

Agape Redwood
Co-Founder
Signature Media Group Speakers

John and Deb use *The Submarine Way* to leverage what all organizations should be doing: creating an atmosphere of inclusion and treating their biggest investment, their human capital, with respect. Their examples of the contrasts between the Navy's system of acclimation and the common practices of community/religious organizations and business offices show a clear gap in the way inclusion should be done.

This look at how things are done under the water should emerge as the standard for organizations to follow. What if we actually applied these principles? What if we dared to emulate a system that has been proven to be successful for the past 242 years? We would see a bigger ROI, better trained professionals, more acceptance, more peace, successful missions, and better performance. The barriers that have been used to block progress, and ultimately performance, would be removed.

Are you ready for a mind shift? Get ready to take a ride below the surface and learn The Submarine Way. This system will transform your organization and help you reach the results you've been struggling to achieve.

Freya S. Huffman, MBA, PHR, ABD
Author, Performance Improvement Expert, Motivational Speaker
www.freyamotivates.com

Deb and John's exciting new book on The Submarine Way toward diversity and inclusion will totally change the way you think about a subject that can be a sensitive and challenging one to tackle.

Being a corporate executive, former pastor, and business owner, I've been faced with leading and fostering an inclusive environment and team when the stakes were really high. Their insightful and inspiring approach will be different, yet successful. I encourage you to read it and dive in!

Darryl Webb

Senior Vice President of Operations
Golden Corral Corporation

DIVERSITY
AND
INCLUSION
THE SUBMARINE WAY

DIVERSITY
── AND ──
INCLUSION
THE SUBMARINE WAY

WHAT LIFE UNDERWATER TAUGHT ME ABOUT INCLUSION

DEBORAH CAKE FORTIN, M.S.
JOHN GREGORY VINCENT, M.B.A.
VICE PRESIDENT, PERFORMANCE SOLUTIONS, INTERNATIONAL, EAGLE'S FLIGHT

Published by Advantage, Charleston, South Carolina.
Member of Advantage Media Group.

ADVANTAGE is a registered trademark, and the Advantage colophon is a trademark of Advantage Media Group, Inc.

Printed in the United States of America.

10 9 8 7 6 5 4 3 2 1

ISBN: 978-1-59932-905-5
LCCN: 2017959224

Cover design by Melanie Cloth.
Layout design by George Stevens.

This publication is designed to provide accurate and authoritative information in regard to the subject matter covered. It is sold with the understanding that the publisher is not engaged in rendering legal, accounting, or other professional services. If legal advice or other expert assistance is required, the services of a competent professional person should be sought.

Advantage Media Group is proud to be a part of the Tree Neutral® program. Tree Neutral offsets the number of trees consumed in the production and printing of this book by taking proactive steps such as planting trees in direct proportion to the number of trees used to print books. To learn more about Tree Neutral, please visit **www.treeneutral.com.**

Advantage Media Group is a publisher of business, self-improvement, and professional development books. We help entrepreneurs, business leaders, and professionals share their Stories, Passion, and Knowledge to help others Learn & Grow. Do you have a manuscript or book idea that you would like us to consider for publishing? Please visit advantagefamily.com or call **1.866.775.1696.**

We would like to honor the silent service that taught us the US Navy's system (called The System in the following pages). The navy was good to John when he needed it most. Since John spent thirteen years of his twenty-year career proudly wearing the anchors of a naval chief petty officer, he salutes his brothers and sisters who also wore those anchors. In addition, we would like to recognize the individuals who have touched us and taught us that all of us will always be better than one of us. Here's to new beginnings, fair winds, and following seas.

In my role as mayor of Augusta, one of my goals was to build the community. This sense of community was for the whole of Augusta and inclusion was a priority. In my new role as a radio talk show host, I feature guests who have sometimes been controversial on the public scene, and I help to humanize them in the public eye. This allows listeners to have the proverbial cup of coffee with people they don't know and may not have understood. I feel strongly that if we, as a society, only took the time to look each other in the eyes, open our hearts and minds, and have this cup of coffee, many of the problems our society faces would be addressed with humanity-based solutions, in which everyone wins.

The Submarine Way talks of community as *crew-munity* and believes that crew-munity is a cornerstone of the submarine system. The Submarine Way system is a new, fresh approach. Many of the programs out there today are awareness and training based, teaching affirmative action and equal opportunity. These initiatives are necessary, but moving beyond these to a program that targets inclusion, regardless of whether it is a business, church, or community is next-level thinking. The place society finds itself in today needs next-level thinking.

Mayor Deke Copenhaver
Augusta, Georgia

THE FOULED ANCHOR

The **Fouled Anchor** is the emblem of the Rate of Chief Petty Officer of the United States Navy. The fouled anchor has long been the symbol of the Chief Petty Officer. In terms of the Chief, the fouled anchor symbolizes the trials and tribulations that every Chief Petty Officer must endure on a daily basis. Attached to the Anchor is a length of chain and the letters U.S.N. To the novice, the anchor, chain and letters only identify a Chief Petty Officer of the United States Navy, but, to a Chief, these have a more noble and glorious meaning.

The **"U"** stands for **Unity**, which reminds us of cooperation, maintaining harmony and continuity of purpose and action.

The **"S"** stands for **Service**, which reminds us of service to our God, our fellow man and our Navy.

The **"N"** stands for **Navigation**, which reminds us to keep ourselves on a true course so that we may walk upright before God and man in our transactions with all mankind, but especially with our fellow Chiefs. The Chain is symbolic of flexibility and reminds us of the chain of life that we forge day by day, link by link and may it be forged with Honor, Morality and Virtue.[1]

---

1   "The Chief's Fouled Anchor," *Goat Locker*, accessed October 30, 2017, http://goatlocker.org/cpo. html.

ACKNOWLEDGMENTS

We would like to thank Diane Murphy from Diversity Works for believing we had something important to say that day in November when we first explained The Submarine Way to a large group of people in Florence, South Carolina. And we'd like to thank the people in that room, who stood and cheered for us, their eyes damp with emotion. Many of them followed us out to our car, asking questions and wanting more, because they believed that The Submarine Way to diversity and inclusion could make a difference. They all helped us believe that getting The System out to as many businesses, faith organizations, and communities as possible, in as short a time as possible, could change these organizations for the better. Many of them have become part of our network of believers, who have hired us as consultants and let us do our magic, and we appreciate all of them! Thank you for the vote of confidence.

Thank you also for the opportunity to learn from the organizations we have worked for: The US Navy, ADP, Travelers, and Gallup. We have started, led, and developed diversity teams, and experienced diversity and inclusion at their best at these organizations. Without them we might not have a message or a system that works.

Finally, we say thank you to Captain Brad McDonald and Phil Geldart, two very different leaders with similar messages. You inspire both of us to have faith that there are good leaders who employ inclusion in a practical and realistic way that gets results. Thank you, also, for contributing to the richness of this book. It wouldn't be as powerful without your examples.

ABOUT THE AUTHORS

John Gregory Vincent served on a variety of operational submarines for fourteen of his twenty years of US Navy service, retiring as a command master chief. Since then, John has had a full career in business, owned his own consulting company— the Genesis Group— worked for Gallup as a consultant, and, most recently, joined Eagle's Flight as VP of Performance Solutions, International. The theme across these roles is John's deep understanding of human behavior. Describing himself as a human behavioral junkie, he explains that the petri dish of the submarine, the experiences of his sales team's at CBS, the deep dive into the research learned at Gallup, and the experiential training at Eagle's Flight all have contributed to the richness of his experience and knowledge of human behavior. His belief that true inclusion is possible is grounded in personal experience. As a keynote speaker and advisor for The Submarine Way, John's goal is that tiny little thing called total transformation: transformation of how people interact with, relate to, and include each other. He has no doubt that The System can be successful.

Deb Cake Fortin has been in the business world for more than twenty-five years, managing people, leading diversity teams, starting them, and changing them. Deb has been a VP of operations and client services as well as a general manager in several large organizations. She started her graduate degree twice, and abandoned it both times because it didn't fit her passion. Finally, when a degree came along that fit her passion for measuring and changing human performance, she settled in and got her graduate degree in human performance technology. She has coached and mentored many an individual in life and business. As John did, she saw first-hand that when people have a common goal, the differences fall away. She helped John to see that the system employed by submarines was adaptable to all environments, which led her to found The Submarine Way. Her professional experience of how diversity and inclusion work in the business world has been critical to this book. She and John have an equal passion to change the world. *What if we could all get along?* she asks. Or even better, what if we could all share a mission to change the world?

TABLE OF CONTENTS

PREFACE

This is *not* your standard-issue book on inclusion and diversity. *The Submarine Way* describes a system built on the incredible undersea world of naval submarines and how the diverse people on these silent moving tubes work through their duffle bags of personal biases and meld into an inclusive, mission-focused machine. There will be language you do not understand and language describing key parts of The System that are at least edgy if not flat out uncomfortable to read. But this is The System and it is real. Inclusion is not tolerance. When you have inclusion, you aren't offended by, say, the bad odor of submarines. When you have inclusion, you forget that the smell even exists.

So if you really want to immerse yourself in The Submarine Way, go grab four people you don't like, work yourselves up into a sweaty lather, and then lock yourselves in a small closet with a single flashlight. All set? Now you're ready to dive into The Submarine Way!

THE SUBMARINE WAY

When you saw this book's title, you likely asked yourself what diversity, inclusion, and a submarine have in common. Well, everything.

On a submarine, inclusion is critical to teamwork, to accomplishing mission, to reducing conflict, and to appreciating the strengths of every individual. Without exaggeration, the survival of mankind depends on this concept. As you read on, you will feel our passion for this system as well as our belief that a very different approach to inclusion is required. Just as civil rights legislation followed the evolution of the concept of human rights, a system to ensure inclusion follows the moral belief that inclusion is the right thing to do. There are laws on affirmative action, but do they ensure inclusion? Today, most would say no. In the US Navy, The System was so engrained in our daily life that it felt organic. It can also feel organic in your organization; the most successful processes and systems do.

> When it comes to a system of inclusion, there's none better than the one that takes place on a submarine.

When it comes to a system of inclusion, there's none better than the one that takes place on a submarine. Imagine you are in a 300-

foot-long, fast attack, 637 class submarine—the smallest submarine in the U.S. fleet—with about 110 men, 80 bunks, and no privacy. For the bunk situation to work, once one person gets out of the bunk, another crawls in before the bunk even cools (a bedding arrangement that earned submarine bunks the nickname of hot racks). The reality of life on a submarine is not pleasant, to say the least. The smell of diesel fuel and body odor is everywhere and the surroundings can shift between petri dish to powder keg, depending on the mission. The state of emotion might be fear, or it might be pure boredom, and getting from point A to point B is the sole purpose of the next few days. Then there's superstition. All sailors are superstitious.

In fact, the two dolphins on either side of all submarine insignia are there to represent the sailors' superstition that if a dolphin or two are jumping in the bow wake, the mission will go well.

Now imagine being on this small sub with a crew mate who annoys you and whom you try to avoid. Imagine sharing 300 feet of cramped space, and a rack, and seeing that person multiple times a day, and, maybe, sharing a watch. How do you think that might go?

I won't give away the secret to The System now, but believe it or not, the situation I just described will probably be handled well and, maybe, even better than well.

Why does this completely unpredictable life in a cramped space with few amenities create lifelong fans of life on a submarine despite massive differences in personality? The secret is in the sauce. Please read on.

One of the things that has become clear to me about life on a submarine is that norms (actions that support a strong sense of community, or as we submariners call it, crew-munity), and governance are critical to the effective operation of a submarine. The message here is that these characteristics are necessary for the successful operation of everything. There aren't always a lot of norms in the business setting, or, strangely enough, in the community setting either. It is strange to imagine that a community doesn't have community, but it happens. Think about your own neighborhood, for instance. Do you know who lives a couple houses down from you? When was the last time you said hi to your neighbors? Have you ever shared a meal with them?

Why does this completely unpredictable life in a cramped space with few amenities create lifelong fans of life on a submarine despite massive differences in personality? The secret is in the sauce.

Unfortunately, it often takes tragic events for a sense of community to emerge.

Think about disasters such as Hurricanes Katrina and Harvey, or 9/11. After Hurricane Harvey, Texans of all colors and sizes waded through water to rescue their neighbors. Their can-do and won't-be-defeated attitude was felt by everyone viewing the news media. During 9/11, New York firemen and police went way beyond the normal scope of their job to rescue their fellow New Yorkers, and many gave their lives in the process. The spirit those communities conveyed inspired the rest of the country.

What if it didn't take a tragedy to inspire a sense of community in a community? What if there were a system that, once executed, created the *inclusion* necessary for a true community? This book is intended to help you understand more about what is meant by community, leadership, and the structures that support the community, and most importantly, to understand The System that leads to inclusion, which is key to building a true sense of community.

> **My natural appreciation for the norms that contribute to community, and lead to inclusion has influenced everything I do with my clients.**

It has been many years since I served on a submarine, but the life lessons my naval service taught me have stuck with me over the years, from starting my own consultancy in human behavior to working for Gallup, and, more recently, Eagle's Flight. My natural appreciation for the norms that contribute to community, and lead to inclusion has influenced everything I do with my clients. I often use a predictable, repeatable system when I consult with my clients. What I have learned is that without inclusion, a team cannot have synergy. And without synergy, a team cannot focus on its mission, whether that mission is to navigate the Atlantic in the execution of a Cold War exercise, or whether it is to improve engagement in a Fortune 500 company.

As an entrepreneur, I successfully used this system until I met a woman who, originally, was a client—yes, let's get it out there: I married my client—she has been an impressive addition to my company. When Deb and I met, I had just started a consulting company after leaving my first post-navy job. Deb helped me with a mission statement and business plan, and years later, she became an impressive life partner—but I digress. Deb Cake Fortin, my Deb, after more than twenty-five years of leading people and running organizations with a focus on improved engagement, is a convert to this system. She teaches it and has identified the intricacies I missed. I thought inclusion was coincidental until she identified the details of The System, clarifying it for me. Deb is a coauthor of this book because she pulled it out of my head and put it on paper. We have a mission to change the companies we work with, ignite communities, build bridges in neighborhoods, and yes, change the world. It's a tiny little goal, but we are optimistic. Follow us on this journey as we explore life on a submarine, but even more importantly, as we explore what life underwater can teach us about inclusion. Take a deep breath as we slip under the waves.

PART I

THE WHY AND HOW OF THE SUBMARINE WAY

CHAPTER 1

DO IT THE SUBMARINE WAY

Most of us came to the US Navy with our duffle bags full of biases and issues. We came from very different backgrounds. Some of us came from wealthy families and joining the navy was a great way to punish Mom and Dad who objected to this choice of career. Others came because this was their only hope of an education and future. There were southerners, Asians, African Americans, and even a few New Yorkers, like me. For some, the shoes they put on in basic training were the first brand-new pair of shoes they'd ever owned.

Some of these biases were recognized by the Sailors and some of them were not, but the minute they went down the hatch and the second their feet hit the steel deck, those biases and prejudices became irrelevant. Individual differences fell away and mission and purpose replaced them. That is The Submarine Way.

Deb's experience with bias in the workplace paralleled my own in the submarine force. When mission and purpose in a corporate setting were clear, bias took a backseat, and inclusion and mission success were the result.[2]

> **The second their feet hit the steel deck, those biases and prejudices became irrelevant. Individual differences fell away and mission and purpose replaced them. That is The Submarine Way.**

If we can make life work in submarines, why do we struggle so much with differences in society at large? Why do we get hung up on whom others love, whom others marry, or who's a member of the country club? The answer goes back to our duffle bags full of biases. I heard a wise speaker on diversity once say that "if you have a brain, you have biases." The answer to this is not whether we have them or not, but what we do with them. Do we need to act on everything we think or feel? Of course not. We have that evolved frontal lobe to help us cope with the uncomfortable or different. Did those brand-new sailors just shove their biases into a deep, dark corner? No, because tolerance is only one step on the way to inclusion and tolerance can only last for so long. Did they get assimilated into a new norm when their feet hit the steel deck? No, because assimilation also means stifling one's talents and strengths, which is unhealthy.

---

2   Deb recalls a time when she was traveling with her insurance company employer as a regional VP, working with independent agents to improve loss ratio and increase sales. They had clear goals, a clear mission, and even when some of the agents decided the new goals didn't work for them and deselected themselves, the remaining agents were very engaged. Sales increased, even without the agents who left, and without the agents who were contributing to the poor loss ratios, the loss ratios improved. The group that remained became tight, a crew-munity. The fact that women were very new to this part of the business world became irrelevant.

No, what happened was that inclusion quickly became a way of life because, on a submarine, every strength is needed, and I mean *every*. So, there you have it, The Submarine Way.

THE SYSTEM

On a fast attack submarine, 110 men navigate, run a nuclear reactor, cook, serve, clean, maintain and fix equipment, and stand a watch, 24/7. And despite being in a very crowded space, these 110 young men (submariners are rarely older than thirty) get along, accomplish difficult missions, and manage to put out fires, as well as fight the bad guys. How do these very junior (by business standards) sailors welcome new crew and make sure there's professional development (qualification and training) for everyone, as well as create an inclusive environment? Because of The System that exists in The Submarine Way.

> Inclusion quickly became a way of life because, on a submarine, every strength is needed, and I mean *every.*

As I mentioned earlier, life on submarines developed a natural appreciation in me for the norms that lead to community, and in my post-navy career I employed these norms with my clients. But when Deb helped me look objectively at what we did well, we realized it could be systematized.

Of course, as a junior enlisted, I didn't realize my approach constituted a system when I was first introduced to it. It felt unmethodical, but as the years went on, I saw the same system rolled out, repeatedly, with the same result. Mission and purpose became the focus and inclusion became the result, and the result was critical on submarines because every three years, everyone changed out.

What would the result be if your entire company, church, or community changed every three years? The pastor, the secretary of the church, the assistant pastor, and every church member were brand-new every three years? Or the CEO, vice presidents, managers, and associates were different every three years at your business? Most would see that as chaos. The reality on the submarine, however, was that chaos did not follow. Order, mission, purpose, qualification, and, almost immediately, inclusion prevailed. Let's add an additional complicating factor. Ten to fifteen of the sailors were straight out of school and only a handful had more than ten years on the job. That being said, there has never been a serious nuclear accident on a submarine. If all of this wasn't complicated enough, add the young age of submariners—only a couple of chiefs, the commanding officer, and executive officer (XO) tend to be older than thirty. Now apply that situation to business. Can you imagine a nineteen-year-old in charge of reporting to the board, or responsible for the P&L? That level of responsibility is similar to that of a young sailor on a submarine. So why can all the normal rules of operation get thrown out the window and the result still be a high-performing and inclusive operation?

If you wonder why your organization struggles with inclusion—and likely struggles with sales goals, margin, or other business metrics—you should solve the inclusion problem and then your organization will experience synergy that benefits the bottom line.

We said the secret was in The System. Well, here it is: The System is a step by step, repeatable system of inclusion that, by the way, has side benefits in meeting goals and achieving missions. If you wonder why your organization struggles with inclusion—and likely struggles with sales goals, margin, or other business metrics—you should solve the inclusion problem and then your organization will experience synergy that benefits the bottom line.

As each chapter unfolds, the details of The System will be revealed. But first, here's a quick overview of The System's critical components of inclusion.

Check-In: A system of onboarding so robust that upon completion, crewmembers (business associates) have everything they need to do their job, including tools, contacts, and familiarity with the environment. They also understand their unique contribution to the success of the mission. They are welcomed in the most practical way, according to their contribution. This system is completely and totally performance based.

Crew-Munity: This is a healthy team wherein individual strengths blend into a synergistic fighting machine, whether the fight is for revenue, client satisfaction, or fighting the bad guys at sea.

Everyone matters, if they contribute: This is the process of identifying team members' unique contributions, providing the training to make sure they are successful, and then holding them accountable for their results. Having high levels of accountability during training is key (keeping in mind that the training never ends), and sailors quickly understand that they have no place on board if they are not contributing. It is that tough and it is that clear to every sailor.

Choose an Ombudsman: An official liaison to the command, the ombudsman takes the pulse of the crew-munity. In the business world, ombudsmen have direct access to the most senior leaders of the organization. The System will not work if these individuals do not have authority to drive change. Ombudsmen are not a figurehead, but an integral part of the team. They need to have high-ranking status. In the submarine world, if ombudsmen call, the commander takes that call.

Focus on the mission: This involves a clear understanding of the overall goals of the organization and individuals' specific and daily contribution to those goals. Do all employees in your organization understand its mission and what their contribution to it is, every day? If not, walk around and take an informal pulse of your organization. My guess is that you will be shocked at what you hear.

Along with a discussion of The System in Part I, in Part II we'll talk about the other components necessary to anchor—yes, a little nautical humor—The System on a submarine, or to maintain it in a business or community. Good leadership is critical (a topic we discuss in chapter 8, titled "Captain of the Ship"), but did you know that professional development, and training and qualification are also critical? This is spelled out in chapter 7, titled "Drill, Drill, Drill." Finally, chapter 9, titled "Don't Get Bilged on Your Own Anchor," uses an old nautical term to deep dive into what can happen when The System breaks down: the results can be deeply disturbing, so beware, and honor The System.

In the chapters ahead, we explore each step in The System and the anchors you need to keep The System in place. We also have "Tactical Readiness" sections and "Deep Dive" questions to help you use The System to guide the leadership and inclusion needs of your business, faith organization, and community.

THREE BASICS TO KNOW BEFORE DIVING INTO THE SUBMARINE WAY

Before we go to chapter 2, titled "Check-In", you'll want to open your duffle bag, stuff those biases and issues into a corner, and pack three basic concepts and the first tactical readiness tool you need to do it The Submarine Way.

1. Even an Imperfect Entity Can Exemplify Inclusion

The military, of course, isn't faultless. Throughout its history it's been involved in segregation of all kinds—women and men, blacks and whites—along with issues of inequality. When the military allowed African American women to join the Women's Army Corp (WAC) because they needed nurses, for instance, those nurses' housing and rations standards were below those of their Caucasian counterparts.

In large part, submarines managed to escape this kind of segregation except for when it came to allowing women to serve. The spoiler alert here is that women have limited roles on submarines today, not because there's deliberate segregation but because no one has completely figured out the accommodation issue. It has been figured out, somewhat, for officers, but enlisted women are still not fully integrated in submarines because of the accommodation challenges. African Americans served on subs almost as soon as submarines were employed by the military. From WWII through the 1970s, African Americans, technically, only served on submarines as stewards, but in reality they did everything. They had to. No one can get away with doing just one thing on a sub. To understand how

> No one can get away with doing just one thing on a sub.

impractical it would be for a crew member to have only one job, you first need to understand the makeup of a submarine, which leads us to the second basic concept.

2. You Always Have a Greater Purpose Than Just Your Job Description

Each submariner does dozens of things necessary to the boat's operation. Before boarding a submarine, new crew members must qualify in their specialty as well as in *submarine watch*, which includes becoming fully trained in damage control. Becoming proficient in damage control means you put another check in the column referring to surviving a disaster. A steward only trained in serving food puts everyone at risk. For example, if a fire were to break out, it would have to be taken care of *right away*, or the whole boat could explode. (In an environment where you have to make your own oxygen, fires are a big fear. Find out more in chapter 7). The same goes for learning the major electrical and mechanical systems. Everyone's talents and skills are needed to operate a submarine, and everyone needs to know how to pitch in when something goes wrong.

See how it doesn't make sense for someone to only be a steward? Every ethnicity has always been fully integrated in the operation of a submarine because it's necessary. Every life on board depends on it.

> **We mentioned earlier about professional development and training leading to qualification. Qualification is the great equalizer and it's a critical part of The System.**

We mentioned earlier about professional development and training leading to qualification. Qualification is the great equalizer and it's a critical part of The System because it applies directly to the concept that all crew members matter if they contribute. On the submarine, there is a specific time frame within which you need to qualify, and if you don't, you don't stay onboard. That is, if you aren't qualified to do your job, you can't contribute and thus serve no purpose. So why keep you on the boat?

Back to our analogy of the sailor hitting the steel deck, everyone feels this interdependence of strengths from the moment they come onboard because they understand the mission: everyone is responsible for fighting the submarine and all crew members have to do their job well to make that happen. How does this translate to your business, faith organization, or community? All employees need to feel important and they need to know their job is important. Every job and every individual is necessary in fighting the submarine, even if that role is to bake fresh cookies for the sailors. On the submarine, the fact that every person and every job matters isn't just a slogan, or a mission statement that was read once a year. In fact, it's rarely vocalized; it's simply understood. And when it's clear, we put another check in the survival column.

3. Direct Communication Leads to Inclusion

Doing your job on a submarine sometimes means you're working in one of the most inherently disrespectful environments on Earth. In the close living quarters of submarines, issues of disrespect, such as talking too loudly while someone is trying to sleep or study, are not brought to the chief to resolve. The individuals involved resolve it right there, with direct and usually colorful metaphors. The offending sailor immediately becomes quiet and peace is maintained.

How did we get disrespect to lead to respect? It's a twofold answer. First, in today's business culture, we say we're good at crucial conversations. Such conversations are direct and clear, and don't leave room for misinterpretation. This direct and open communication is respected.

Second, you are respected if you contribute, work hard, and add value. That's it. The fact that you are white, black, gay, or whatever, makes no difference—and yes, we all know about gay men on submarines. No one cares about any of that as long as they do their job—and they do. Those who don't add value are reprimanded. For instance, when I served on a submarine, while new sailors were qualifying for submarine watch, others stayed up to take their watch. If the new sailors took their time or were lazy in qualifying, that disrespect generated pure anger in the sailors who were covering their watch because the new sailors were not contributing to fighting the submarine. To avoid that disrespect, new sailors received a lot of help in qualifying. (More to follow on that in later chapters.)

On a submarine, every individual has a purpose, and every individual has strengths, some of which might not even be related to that individual's formal role. For instance, even though my formal role on the submarine was that of assistant navigator, one of my strengths was in providing entertainment. I have a quick wit, a good vocabulary, and back then, salty language. See how my contribution went beyond my job as assistant navigator? One by one, the new sailors would pit their wits against mine, saying the most outrageous things and then glancing at each other to see if their remarks had hit home. There was almost always laughter, but glances back and forth, and then at me, told me that they knew this young sailor was going to get his lunch eaten, and eat his lunch I did. Nothing was sacred—girlfriends, jobs, assumed education, intelligence—everything except our biases. Again, those biases didn't go anywhere; they just didn't have a place on the submarine.

This jocular disrespect was one of the ways I earned respect from the other sailors. Counterintuitive, I know, but when inclusion is in place, things that may sound like disrespect, such as conversations that can sound argumentative to those unfamiliar with them (*direct conversations*), can lead to much deeper levels of respect, a topic that we'll dive into a little more in short order.

THE SUBMARINE WAY'S NUMBER-ONE TACTICAL READINESS TOOL: OPEN COMMUNICATION

Too often we avoid direct conversations that lead to clarity. We beat around the bush, avoiding obvious issues such as an unengaged workforce or turnover instead of having a direct conversation about them long before they start to manifest in very negative ways.

What would happen in a community if a cop, known to get rough with people in his community, had peer after peer tell him, directly and clearly, how detrimental his actions were to the community? And what would happen if he were not to

> **In the submarine force, there's a high level of self-regulation and peer regulation.**

listen to them, and the entire community were to react by putting pressure on him? That's exactly what happens on a submarine. In the submarine force, there's a high level of self-regulation and peer regulation, which can be very effective. Now imagine a peer-regulated business in which workers decide what is acceptable behavior, and accepted norms regulate behavior long before there's an issue. What a powerful way that would be to get things done quickly and address issues that could be detrimental to the community.

Open communication is the best tool to foster inclusion. When I served on a submarine, if we weren't sleeping or taking some "alone" time (usually in front of everyone and with only headphones for a barrier), we talked about everything. It didn't matter what our social or ethnic background was. We all worked together, slept together, ate together, and shared some of life's most wonderful events—and tragic events. When a crew member received word that a relative had died, that person reached out to whoever was nearest to talk about it. We didn't look for a white face, a black face, or someone with a similar accent to ours. We all supported each other. There was no formal education about inclusion, but our informal education produced norms so strong that no one crossed them. As tough as that environment was—and it was brutal—there was support and inclusion. All crew members were worthwhile if they contributed to fighting the submarine.

Businesses that want to tackle more effective communication, reduce conflict, and create better team synergy and inclusion use crucial techniques to guide difficult conversations to positive outcomes. Clearly, tough conversations in business or in communities need to be tactful but direct. If tactful doesn't do the trick, however, throw polite out the window and be direct. A little bit of edge to the communication isn't always a bad thing. For example, Deb and I have a unique relationship in that we have been consultant and client, business partners, and peers, and now husband and wife.

> **If tactful doesn't do the trick, however, throw polite out the window and be direct. A little bit of edge to the communication isn't always a bad thing.**

We have learned to have direct conversations about our business interests, our personal interests, and those areas that overlap. We start out polite but, when needed, we can be very direct. Suffice it to say, there is not much left to fester. Communication on a submarine takes many different forms. In my years off the sub, I have effectively practiced these communication techniques at home and in my business. Perfected on the sub, they kept our focus on the result, not on our differences. **From embracing silence to understanding how listening and feedback skills can enhance overall stress management, the following are the four parts of crucial conversations.**

1. Silence Can Contribute to Better Communication

Breaking off a conversation and allowing silence is usually an attempt to get someone to open up. This was especially true on the submarine on which I served. A letter from home, a butt-chewing from a senior officer or a chief, or some other event causing a disturbance in the normal rhythm of the boat would be followed by silence, which played an effective role in shutting down the banter and creating an opportunity for a different kind of interaction.

Over the years, Deb has noticed that organizational teams that are comfortable enough to be silent with each other are those most likely to have moved on to norming. This shows a respect for, or a sensitivity to, a need for privacy, concentration, and/or personal space. Teams that report minor infractions to their supervisor—for example, someone bringing in a radio and playing it too loud—do not yet have the trust to communicate with each other. If I am happy or annoyed with someone, I need to directly tell that person. This is almost a lost art in the business world. It might not be an inclusion issue in terms of diversity, but developing sensitivity in communication can improve and accelerate the inclusion process.

2. Really Listen: The Biggest Breakdowns Occur When Listening Stops

Back on the submarine, listening was the antidote to having a family far away and, sometimes, months out, cramped quarters, and boredom. Listening seems like a pretty basic communication technique, but there's more to it than just using your ears. It is really about giving full attention to the person who is talking to you so you can offer a coherent response that improves communication.

3. Feedback: An Important Part of a Completed Communication System

Feedback, or acknowledgment, is necessary to complete the communication loop. It can be done by either providing feedback or listening to feedback so messages can be modified. When I served on a submarine, feedback was brutal, direct, honest, and, sometimes, not pleasant, but there was zero tolerance for communication breakdown while you stayed focused on accomplishing the mission. On the rare occasion when feedback did not happen, communication broke down and, every once in a while, led to a bow diesel conflict (a very rare type of conflict resolution, which I discuss further in chapter 6).

4. Stress Management: Crucial Conversations Can Relieve Stress

Potential causes of stress were everywhere on the submarine, from cramped space and lack of privacy to not seeing the outside world for long periods of time. To manage the stress of cramped space, I would sometimes imagine that the submarine was the whole world and when I walked from one end to the other, it was so far, I could get winded. Many of us played similar games in our minds to cope with a situation no human beings can fully cope with until they experience it. Those who allowed the space, the dark, the fear, and the lack of privacy to get to them were often those who did not have coping skills for dealing with stress.

FIVE STEPS TO DEALING WITH STRESS

What are your coping skills when you are under stress? Do you have good tools for managing and diffusing it, or is stress sitting in your system and eating away at you? If you have not figured out how to handle stress, start building some tools today.

1. **Set ground rules, listen, and understand each other's point of view:** When I served on a submarine, we had very clear ground rules, the most important being that a conflict should never appear to be personal. This was

---

different from two people picking on each other, when nothing is sacred. Conflict was never confused with a clash of personalities, personal backgrounds, or religious affiliations. Period. Not only was that understanding a ground rule; it was a norm.

2. **Describe the conflict from all points of view:** This was almost always the case, even if the description of the conflict was loud and colorful. There was always an audience, but unless the conflict was a group issue, the two arguing the issue were the only ones discussing it at top volume.

3. **Discuss the options:** Brainstorming solutions was critical. Nothing could get in the way of the success of the mission. The critical element was not to leave the issue or conflict unresolved. As we stated earlier, festering issues create more problems and the best way to avoid those is with direct discussions.

4. **Determine the next steps:** The next steps were often discussed at top volume until all parties agreed to them. Sometimes, these were simple next steps, such as allowing time before the next discussion. When a mentor (we submariners called mentors sea daddies) had a new sailor who was not keeping up with watch training, the only resolution was to get back on track. No other resolution was acceptable.

5. **Discuss the issue again if the first discussion didn't produce results:** This rarely happened,

but lack of clarity was sometimes at the root of the issue and circling back could produce the calm and the reflection necessary to clear up the situation. All of us wanted the other sailors to be successful. Interdependence was so great that when one of us failed, we all failed.

WHO IS FIGHTING THE SUBMARINE IN YOUR ORGANIZATION?

When social groups can communicate clearly and work together for a common goal, differences fall away. Remember the analogy of feet hitting the steel deck and differences falling away, being replaced with mission and purpose? I saw this happen again and again on different subs, and I've seen it successfully implemented numerous times in business.

In your organization, who is fighting the submarine? Are you sending a strong message about norms and the value of every contributing member? Norms that create a standard pattern of social behavior? And contribute to culture which are all of these attitudes, customs and norms. If not, education won't work, resource groups won't work, and talk of tolerance won't work. Start by communicating a very strong message of norms and zero tolerance for behaviors outside this set of values—more on that in chapter 2. When you put social groups together and give them common goals such as fighting wars or building houses for the community, prejudice and bias break down and inclusion is the result.

DEEP DIVE

THREE QUESTIONS ON CREATING DIVERSITY AND INCLUSION IN YOUR ORGANIZATION

Why can all the normal business rules of operation get thrown out the window and the result is a high-performing and inclusive operation? Ask your organization the following diversity-and-inclusion-focused questions to assess the likelihood you are building the foundation for inclusion:

1. Do you hire the young and inexperienced, teaching them what you expect from them?

2. Do you hire based on skills and strengths, first with blind interviews to ensure you are hiring based on skill and experience? (A little news here: the day of face-to-face interviews, exclusively, is dead. They mask our ability to identify talent with too many sensory inputs.)

3. Are you open to the contributions of a wide variety of skills, personalities, and strengths?

The answer to how these things can be effective at creating a high-performing and inclusive operation is The System. Batten the hatches and rig for dive. This book will change everything you think you know about diversity and inclusion.

CHAPTER 2

CHECK-IN: THERE'S JUST ONE CHANCE TO MAKE A FIRST IMPRESSION

C heck-in is the first piece of The System. In the business world, my experience with check-in—also known as onboarding— was never as welcoming or as well set up for success as it was on the submarine. The one exception was my onboarding at Eagle's Flight. The power of a positive onboarding cannot be stressed enough. Most of the time, prior to Eagles Flight, I often wondered if I had made a mistake, literally on my first day of work. At Eagle's Flight, on my first day in their dog-friendly, Canadian culture, I was welcomed, along with my Siberian husky, Rufus.

The CEO greeted me and proceeded to feed my dog treats as he talked to me. He literally knelt and hugged Rufus while never breaking stride in his welcoming conversation with me. I will talk more about that remarkable man, Phil Geldart, later in chapter 7,

but making both of us feel welcome—yes, my dog too—was his priority that day (and I found out later that Siberian huskies are his favorite dogs). That day I felt I had come home, as I had all those years earlier on a submarine. The other thing that Phil did for me as part of my onboarding was to set up dinners at the homes of key business contributors so that I could meet their wives and children and get to know everyone socially. You will learn later that Phil has figured out check-in and crew-munity, and displays much of The System from The Submarine Way. He is even a pretty darn good ombudsman.

We all want to feel valued. In business, the best time for that is as soon as possible during the check-in or onboarding process.

You don't have to have a dog-friendly culture to make people feel welcome or appreciated at your office, but remember the number-one characteristic we human beings have in common: we all want to feel valued. In business, the best time for that is as soon as possible during the check-in or onboarding process. Remember that as soon as the new sailor's feet hit the steel deck, biases are replaced with mission. Check-in is a critical piece of this transition.

On the submarine, check-in is taken seriously. It entails leadership accountability, but everyone has a role. Check-in sets the stage for everything. Another thing to note is that no matter how many years of experience you have, or what your rank is—including commanding officers and XOs—you still go through a check-in process. If the boat is similar to one you have served on before, it might be an abbreviated check-in, but, nevertheless, check-in is for everyone.

On the submarine, check-in is taken seriously. It entails leadership accountability, but everyone has a role. Check-in sets the stage for everything.

To set the stage, check-in for new sailors always starts with sub school. For me, sub school was at Navy Base New London, in Connecticut. I spent about eight weeks there and graduated top of my class. I was motivated by my desire to be on a fast attack based out of San Diego or Pearl Harbor. I was told that being a number-one graduate went a long way toward ensuring I would get my choice of base and boat, but no such luck. Not only did my orders indicate I would serve on a missile boat, but my base was in Charleston, South Carolina. I love Charleston and the south now, but for a boy from New York City, bars that closed on Sunday were a cultural shock. I could write much more on that topic, but enough said.

The difference between receiving an offer letter from a new employer and deployment orders after training is significant. When you leave training at the navy base, you get your orders, details on where to report, directions to the base, and details on where your family can get information and support during your deployment.

You even get the name of someone submariners call a sponsor. This is a person you can ask for when you get to the boat, and whom you can also call before arrival if you need something. This is just the start. The richness of the information and the send-off is beyond anything I have experienced in the private sector. So, compare the navy's deployment orders to that corporate offer letter with not much more to it than your start date and, maybe, your expected arrival time, title, and salary. When you start serving on your first boat, you are truly set up for success.

CHECK-IN: DAY ONE

The first step in the check-in process is the assignment of someone who will walk the new sailor through the process. This person's responsibility is to deliver a good check-in experience from both the leaders' and the new sailor's perspective. During check-in, the new sailor gets a tour of the boat, mess deck, head, and berthing. Then he's introduced to the critical crew members: the captain, XO, and other officers. After check-in, the sailor has all the basic materials and equipment needed to begin the qualification process. Remember how qualification is the great equalizer? During my check-in everyone was very nice, almost personal, but no one was that nice to me again until I qualified, because qualification meant you were contributing, and contributing is critical to the success of the mission.

> **During my check-in everyone was very nice, almost personal, but no one was that nice to me again until I qualified, because qualification meant you were contributing, and contributing is critical to the success of the mission.**

Check-in on a submarine for about ten new sailors in 300 feet of space takes over a week. If your organization has 50,000 employees, your onboarding should last close to a month. It doesn't need to be continuous, but pulling associates back in for follow-up onboarding once they are familiar with the basics is how you build continuity and relationships. If your company has 2,000 employees, then a solid week of onboarding to build relationships, provide context, and create a basic understanding of the culture and people is necessary. During the submarine check-in process, new sailors will spend time with over twenty other sailors, and meet over thirty more, all significant to their success. How many critical players do your new employees interact with during onboarding?

My check-in experience on the USS *Bancroft* was the most memorable. I received a check-in card that needed to be signed by everyone who had been involved in my check-in, and what happened next was very different from business onboarding. I was surprised that instead of a formal greeting, such as "I am the corpsman. You come to me when you are very, very sick," many people talked to me and asked me about my background and family. I seemed to matter to everyone I talked to. Did I get the card signed? I sure did and it was a very welcoming process. Although I was the most junior person on board the *Bancroft*, part of my check-in was to attend dedicated meetings with the commanding officer and the XO. Both were truly interested in me and were very welcoming, and that was the last time anyone was nice to me until I qualified for watch.

YOUR ORGANIZATION'S CHECK-IN

Businesses call check-ins onboarding and faith organizations call them the new member or visitor process. Although communities sometimes give newcomers a welcome package, they do more to make newcomers feel that moving into them is difficult. Every water-turn-on service is different, and waiting in line for a new license is a pain. Joining a new community is—let's put it this way—not something you really look forward to doing. If we agree that the check-in is critical to the success of the sailor, then how does this process fit into a community, faith organization, or company? How could your community or business make sure others feel welcome?

TACTICAL READINESS: CHECK-IN QUESTIONS FOR BUSINESSES, FAITH ORGANIZATIONS AND COMMUNITIES

Businesses

Companies are starting to pay more attention to onboarding new associates, but this process is still not given the priority it deserves. Deb remembers being hired into a senior executive position and waiting in the lobby for over an hour on her first day before anyone came out to get her. As someone who had the opportunity to change the onboarding process, she took note of this experience so she could address it later. A new employee's first day is your company's first opportunity to build a good impression. Is the human resource staff member who is responsible for onboarding upbeat and positive? Do new hires get to meet all of the key players, or are they at least given a review of the organization chart, structure, key players, and a mission statement? Are new hires given a tour and is everyone in the company asked to smile, and to be upbeat and positive during that time? Are mentors assigned to cover a new hire's first thirty days to answer the myriad of questions that surface? Most importantly, do new hires know when they will be paid and what they need to do to get paid, and are you sure there will be no slip-ups in their payment procedure? Going back to that old saying that there's only one opportunity to form a first impression, I've known many people who decided to resign from an organization on their day of onboarding. Take it seriously.

Faith Organizations

When prospective members first visit your faith organization, how are they treated? Do they get the obligatory visitor package and fill out a card, never to hear from your organization again unless they initiate contact? Or worse, does your organization approach those who only fit the image you're trying to portray while not approaching those who are different? What if every single visitor had the same experience: a tour of the facility before or after worship and an introduction to key individuals, including the leader? And then, what if there were always a follow-up phone call to visitors, inviting them to a lunch, or a monthly men's or women's meeting? And what if this happened so many times that they felt incredibly welcomed and included? Not every situation will turn out to be positive. Some visitors will feel such an approach is intrusive, but if they are assured the goal is to make them feel welcome, they will understand. The important elements in making someone feel welcome might vary with each house of worship, but onboarding is critical regardless of the specifics.

For instance, the church I attend today provides a welcome basket and a loaf of sweet bread on the first day. New members are asked to stand during the service so they can be welcomed and time is spent shaking hands and giving blessings to one another during the service. The minister of this small southern church has a vision that his congregation will be diverse, so he reaches out to the community and welcomes those who are different. Differences such as ethnic background and race are irrelevant. The minister also spends time helping the community through community outreach and assistance. It is a small start, but the spark is starting to catch.

Communities

Is there a way to make your community more inclusive? Let's take this question to the most basic level: your neighborhood. What do you control that would make your neighborhood more inclusive? How do you make new neighbors feel included? Neighborhoods band together for garage sales, neighborhood watches, and kids' birthday parties, but apart from that, the average neighborhood looks more like a disparate group of individuals who happen to live in the same place. The days of being comfortable with borrowing coffee or a cup of sugar are gone. But what if neighborhoods were welcoming places where neighbors happily rotated making a casserole for the new neighbors on move-in day? What if they stopped by and told new neighbors a little about the area, such as where the best grocery stores are and how to find the playground so that they felt welcome? Would this make your neighborhood more inclusive? Even if the new neighbors weren't very sociable, they would still appreciate the outreach and a community would begin to form. And what about the community itself? If applications for utilities, licenses, or tags are cumbersome and public services are built only as revenue generators and not geared to welcoming new citizens, what can you do to make those first experiences positive?

DEEP DIVE

SIX QUESTIONS TO EVALUATE YOUR CHECK-IN PROCESS

Building a thorough and positive check-in process helps to build inclusion in your faith organization, community, or business. Without one, you could be contributing to company turnover. New members, or associates, could feel excluded because of lack of attention or even offensive practices. This is why check-in is critical.

Evaluate your check-in process with the following questions:

1. Do you survey those who go through the check-in process at your organization to evaluate their experience?

2. If not, how do you know that new people feel welcome? If the answer is that you do not know, a check-in survey is necessary.

    - Check-in questions could include the following:

      - Did you receive the needed tools to get started on your first day?

      - Do you feel welcome in the organization/ community?

      - Do you know the individuals critical to your community or to your role in the organization? Do you know the mission of your organization?

3. How quickly are necessary changes made to your organization's check-in process? If the mission statement, or the president, changes, does your check-in process adapt?

4. How often is the check-in process reviewed? It should be reviewed three times more often than all other processes.

5. Is your check-in process evaluated with an objective eye, with no desire to protect status quo?

6. A single individual should be responsible for the check-in experience in each community or organization. Who is in charge of check-in at your organization?

CHAPTER 3

CREW-MUNITY: PUTTING SOCIAL GROUPS TOGETHER

mmediately upon entering a submarine, I knew I was part of something larger. I could hear it in the crew's conversations when they shared family stories, commiserated over the news of an ill parent or child, or talked about the activities they had enjoyed on the last trip home. Social events were critical to building bonds. When we went to sea, our families relied on each other. We were our own little village, and we felt safe in knowing that our families were there for each other while we were away. When we came back, we enjoyed time together too, holding informal events such as softball games for the family and children's face painting. We even had a game called beer ball, which was, basically, softball with kegs. Running out of balls was okay, but not running out of beer.

Wives and children were always part of these socials and there were predeployment briefs, which family members were encouraged to attend and which reassured us that those left ashore had a solid support structure. The new sailor heard these stories and often looked forward to joining this new extended crew. If you helped to fight the submarine, or if you were a part of the family that supported the sailors, then difference didn't matter; you were a part of the crew-munity.

Being a part of the crew-munity also means having an unofficial purpose that helps to keep the crew-munity together. My unofficial purpose, for instance, was keeping the cooks happy. They had a tough job with limited fresh food. But a good meal always had a way of making us feel better about the cramped quarters we were living in, sometimes for months. Often, after my watch, I would stop by the galley where my favorite cook would have a pizza or fresh cookies waiting for me. This did two things: I got yummy cookies and the cook got genuine appreciation for his work from someone he respected.

My other unofficial role, as I mentioned earlier, was that of a comedian, which served as a coping mechanism for the pressure, confinement, closeness, and boredom of our lives. Not taking yourself, or others, too seriously can be a very important antidote to pressure. Football players slap each other on the backside and throw their heads back and laugh between plays in order to release pressure. Always keeping a sense of humor, allowing yourself to be picked on, and even setting yourself up to take a fall can provide the comic relief needed to break up a tense situation. Laughter relieves stress as well as connects people. When I served on submarines, we tried not to make personal issues the source of our laughter, though we sometimes broke this rule by pointing out idiosyncrasies that drove us crazy about each other. But doing so with humor was necessary to relieve the pressure of close living.

While humor often broke the tension aboard the submarine, what we didn't do, however, was bring up bigotry of any kind; we didn't allow prejudice to cause others to be picked on. We understood and respected boundaries. This was a universal rule of our crew-munity and following it allowed diverse social groups to work together to achieve mission success. This mutual respect for others was the catalyst for true inclusion because it acted as one of the constant unifiers of everyone on board.

CREW-MUNITY AND RESPECTING BOUNDARIES

While all the joking was fun, remember we were on a submarine. The stress, the smells, and the reality that we were never more than about two feet away from someone else created big obstacles, one of which was figuring out personal space. A 2014 Society of Human Resource Managers report on job satisfaction and engagement found that 72 percent of employees rank respectful treatment of all employees as the top factor in job satisfaction. On the sub, respectful treatment had a wide berth. One was respectful of other sailors if they worked hard and contributed to the mission, and they were respectful of other people's ethnicity, sexual orientation, or any other factor that some might consider contentious. For us, respect was, ultimately, about contribution to the mission. Nothing else really mattered.

Captain McDonald, my CO on the USS *L. Mendel Rivers*, liked to say that we didn't do diversity and inclusion training. My minimum expectations were to have the full acceptance of every crew member. Period. For us, respect for the value of every person was needed to complete the mission.

Differences were noticed, of course. They had to be noticed and addressed, but when crew members had a unique skill, performed their job well, and focused on the mission as their priority, then any possible conflict was often quelled. But quelling conflict through direct communication and respecting the contribution of each person did not alleviate the need for sensitivity to personal space, which was one of those boundaries we all maintained to foster crew-munity.

For us, respect for the value of every person was needed to complete the mission.

You don't always know the depth of a ship's keel below the water line, just as you can't know with certainty what someone is thinking or feeling. Along with an excellent system of inclusion, serving on a submarine meant developing a sixth sense about people. In a place where personal space is at a premium (and some would say there wasn't any), respecting all kinds of boundaries kept us harmonious and productive so conflict could not get in the way of the mission. For years, I took those unspoken rules for granted. For example, you didn't pick up someone's magazine lying on a bunk; if a crew member was wearing headphones, you didn't interrupt him. In my fourteen years on operational submarines, I encountered so many of these unwritten expectations about recognizing signals and responding with appropriate behavior that I have probably forgotten most of them.

You don't always know the depth of a ship's keel below the water line, just as you can't know with certainty what someone is thinking or feeling.

Learning to read faces and develop a sixth sense about people helped us navigate (yes, a little sub humor again) the people factor. One memory that is still fresh in my mind was going to the mess deck after watch one day and looking for someone to chat with. I grabbed my coffee and saw my buddy across the room. I started to walk toward him, but when he looked up, we locked eyes, and I immediately knew he needed to be alone. I found another spot to sit and drink my coffee, and soon someone else joined me for conversation. That kind of communication is very subtle but paying attention to the signals, recognizing the need for personal space, and not crossing boundaries kept us focused on the right things. What I discovered during my time on subs, and then in the business world, is that there are five personal space signals that help us navigate small spaces, tense situations, and team dynamics.

FIVE CLUES TO CREW-MUNITY BOUNDARIES

1. **When entering a new space, be clear about what your personal space expectations are.** If listening to loud music in a shared space is not acceptable, be clear but firm about it. Have a conversation about it rather than escalating it. In chapter 1 we talked about clear, direct communication, which is exactly what these situations need. It will avoid leaving the impression there is anything personal about your expectations. Too often, perceived personal slights can be turned into judgments and prejudices that did not start out that way.

2. **Read body language.** When my buddy told me with one look that he didn't want to talk, my ability to sense that was critical. The common characteristic of those inhabitants

of our underwater home we called assholes was that they weren't sensitive to others' needs or concerns. You have to learn how to read faces and expressions. If people extend a hand when you are about to go in for a hug, they are sending you a signal. Do not continue moving toward a hug if you've gotten a negative signal.

3. **Respect physical space boundaries.** Is it okay to slap people on the back or put your arm around them? You have to gauge the situation. You don't always have body language to help you. When upset, some people prefer not to be touched. Others seek out physical comfort. In the submarine space, sensitivity to physical boundaries, such as nudity, has to be maintained to maintain the peace.

4. **Respecting opinion boundaries means being sure about what you believe when faced with a differing opinion.** You should not become defensive when confronted with a different point of view. No matter our similarities, we all have a worldview, and knowing yours and respecting that of others is key. One of the things we did a lot was to pick on each other's point of view, but with no intent to offend. If a crew member could not hold his own in the face of another's opinions, he was going to have a tough day, not to mention a tough six-month deployment. In the end, even those reluctant to share their worldview found their voice, because not having one meant we were not getting the best of everyone risking the mission.

5. **Respecting emotional boundaries means recognizing someone's need for emotional space, including you.** Your emotions belong to you and no one else has responsibility

for them. Knowing your emotional boundaries prevents you from placing blame or accepting blame. On the subs where I served, we had a preoccupation with failure, but the failure of a system or process was not about who was to blame. We took the emotion out of it and approached the issue objectively so that we could identify what needed to change without getting caught up in blame. Don't confuse this with accountability, however. We were very accountable to each other and the mission. We mentioned accountability earlier but will cover it in more detail in chapters 4, 6, and 9.

If you become a student of boundaries, you'll find all kinds of guidelines out there including guidelines on boundaries with children, romantic relationships at work, social boundaries … the list goes on.

Since we were living, working, eating, and socializing all in the same 300 feet of space, we had to apply the rules regarding boundaries in a completely different way. What is at risk if boundaries are crossed in an office environment is compounded on a submarine, where infractions can jeopardize everything. Consider personal space, for instance. There are guidelines on behavior in the personal space between a man and a woman, or between two men, guidelines on professional versus romantic behavior, and guidelines on behavior when cultural and foreign/ethnicity differences are involved, and so on.

In my days of submarine service, women didn't serve full-time on a crew, so female/male personal space was not usually an issue. (Today, women serve on submarines, which now puts this issue in play.) My experience of working with all-female, or largely female, teams in the training command and at Media General have taught me a lot about boundaries with females that I did not need to focus on in my sub days. The general guideline on personal space for male coworkers calls for three to ten feet. If we take 110 men and line them up in a submarine, three feet apart, we are short by ninety feet, so there's no such thing as standard personal space on a sub. How did we cope with the assault on our personal space every day, all day long? The answer to this question is the entire focus of this book: inclusion.

I recall leading a workshop in Washington DC, a few years back. The room was set up with round tables in a space that was too small. From above, the seated participants looked as if they were the teeth of tightly fitting cogs. They were all crammed against their neighbor and almost half of the people in the room had their back to me. I made a joke that, after that day, everyone in the room would be an honorary submariner. To deal with the space issue, I gave more than the normal number of breaks and begged everyone to come back on time. Everyone responded well to the situation, acknowledged the challenge, and made the best of it, but it was clear that this personal

Common Beliefs Regarding Personal Space

Never touch anyone you don't know. Is this a good rule or not? The important rule here is to just be sensitive to body language.

Stay at least three to four feet away from someone if you do not know them well. Need I say more? Smaller offices and submarines don't have that much space.

When someone leans away from you, you are probably in his/her space. Be sensitive to this possibility, but don't jump to conclusions. There are too many cultural differences to assume anything.

Don't lean over anyone's shoulder to read something unless invited. Regardless of the situation, it's always a good idea to ask first before leaning in to read over someone's shoulder.

Don't slap anyone on the back unless you know the person very well. Honestly, I am a big back slapper whether I know you well or not. Always employ instincts around body language and practice strengthening those instincts as often as possible.

space challenge was very difficult. Ironically, this was one of my highest-rated workshops.

THE VIOLATION OF CREW-MUNITY BOUNDARIES AS A TRUST ISSUE

On a submarine, the most serious violation of personal space is stealing. I find it hard to believe, when I look back, that a crew member would dare to steal, sometimes repeatedly, until he was caught. I would venture a guess that most thieves were caught, eventually. The submarine's severest of penalties were enforced on those who stole, and I'm not proud to say that I participated in one of those punishments.

In the case I am recalling, the individual would wait until someone was in the head, with his soap container and towel, waiting to take a shower. The thief would steal the soap and container. He would also steal other little personal articles or toiletries. We began to suspect him because after each incident when soap went missing, he was there. We pieced it together, little by little, and discovered a stash of soap containers and personal items during an inspection. If the thief had needed soap and asked us for it, we would have all given him some. Borrowing was common and considered acceptable. But he never did. Instead, he chose to steal. So we threw him a blanket party.

A blanket party is not fun for the recipient. A navy-issue wool blanket, which is scratchy as hell, is thrown over the crew member's head as he sleeps and three or four men beat him until he has visible bruises and a black eye. The blanket party sends a message to everyone else that 1) this person stole, and 2) he is being punished for his actions. I am not suggesting physical violence is a solution to any problem, but strong norms are. Although stealing happened when I served on submarines, it was quite rare. Since we had very little personal space and few personal items, stealing was more of a trust issue than anything else.

Deb had a similar issue of personal space turning into a trust issue in the business world, and it involved a gate in a parking garage. Two young men, both salespeople reporting to the sales manager who reported to Deb, decided to go out one night and leave their car in the company's parking garage. They had fun hitting popular restaurants and bars in the area, but they got back to the garage so late they found the gate locked and they couldn't get their car out. Out of desperation, they started their car and ran through the gate, severely damaging it. The next morning, neither confessed to the incident, but an investigation revealed that the car and its occupants responsible for the gate crashing were caught on video. The two men were terminated, not because they had crashed through the gate but because they had not faced up to what they had done, creating a much more serious issue: trust. If personal space issues are not dealt with, they can become serious trust issues.

> **Inclusion means that, in your mind, any preconceptions you may have had about personal space no longer exist.**

DON'T JUST TOLERATE STINKY, POOPY SUITS

The issues about personal space are just one example of tolerance versus inclusion. If you were just tolerating other people in your personal space 24/7 on the sub, eventually that tolerance would break. Inclusion, however, means that, in your mind, any preconceptions you may have had about personal space no longer exist.

Of course, tolerance has always been a starting place for diversity and it certainly has its place, but tolerance alone is not enough when tensions are high and the mission is critical, no matter what the mission might be. Tolerance certainly will not allow you to create crew-munity. If we don't appreciate the unique strengths of each member of the team, we miss out on a critical path to success. Tolerance runs out of air when you're 800 feet down (that's the depth I'm officially permitted to cite). There's no room for privacy, and you are with the same men for up to six months. True interdependence, trust, and relationships are the only way to be truly inclusive.

What, then, does tolerance have to do with poopy suits? On the sub, we wore blue jump suits. They were all one piece, which made them easy to put on, but when you went to the head you had to drop them from the shoulders and just let them bunch around your feet. The nickname of poopy suit came about because several times a week, it was resting on the head floor. You had to learn to embrace rather than tolerate a lot concerning the submarine environment, and the head floor was one of them. The smell of poopy suits that had been worn for a few days, body odor (because the distiller was down as much as up and showers were not allowed), the cold, the heat—all of that needed to be embraced or tolerated under pressure—and there was pressure: on the hull, from the mission, and from each other.

On February 1, 2016, *The Huffington Post* published an article titled "Moving beyond Tolerance" by Rev. Victor H. Kazanjian Jr. The minister states he is not a big fan of tolerance as a path to sustainable peace. He goes on to say that tolerance is conflict arrested. He describes it as a great harness applied to the destructive forces of ignorance, fear, and prejudice. We already explored how conflict, when applied correctly, can be a change agent. So, is *arrested conflict,* otherwise known as tolerance, more destructive? In most people's vocabulary, to say you tolerate someone is to imply that your tolerance might end at some point. What I believe the minister is trying to say is if we openly address the issue, we might be able to move beyond tolerance, even risking conflict along the way, to achieve something more. Tolerance is a necessary step toward inclusion, but if it is the only step, inclusion goals are doomed to fail.

Tolerance is conflict arrested.

One of the other things you noticed when your feet hit the submarine's steel deck for the first time was the overall smell of the submarine. It was a combination of body odor, oil, dirty clothes, and, well, I'm not sure of the other smells. John Harding's article titled "Why Submarine Crews Get that Stinking Feeling," published in the *Daily Mail Online* on August 18, 2011, was inspired by the experiences of Danny Danziger, a reporter who spent two weeks on a British sub. Danziger describes that, while he understood the isolation and being cut off from communication with his family, no one warned him about the smell: "As a rough comparison, imagine your teenage son has just come home from three days at the Glastonbury festival where he hasn't washed once. Multiply that by 120 (the number of men in a submarine crew) and think months instead of days, and you begin to get the idea."

I can't say he was wrong about the smell, which was why the first step was to tolerate it and the next was to embrace it. Frankly, I got so comfortable with the smell that I almost forgot about it. Once, when I got off the boat, I dropped my duffle in the garage and forgot about it for a few days until I remembered to unpack and wash my clothes. When I walked into the garage to retrieve them, the smell was overpowering. It's a rough, or maybe smelly, example, but it shows how tolerance is only the first step. When you embrace the differences to the point where you don't even realize they exist, you're well on your way to establishing a state of inclusion.

> **When you embrace the differences to the point where you don't even realize they exist, you're well on your way to establishing a state of inclusion.**

TACTICAL READINESS: CREW-MUNITY QUESTIONS FOR BUSINESSES, FAITH ORGANIZATIONS, AND COMMUNITIES

Faith Organizations

How do you create a crew-munity in your faith organization? How do you create a buzz about activities such as singing in the choir, fund raising for youth organizations, or regular worship functions such as greeting churchgoers and program distribution? Many organizations struggle with getting volunteers for these roles. Singing in the choir, for instance, can be a particularly arduous spot to fill. The elephant in the room is that many faith organizations tend not to be very diverse. How can you attract all types to your church and create a crew-munity? Where do you look for new members? Is it in the same neighborhoods you've always looked? Are your social activities in the community, where your church colors are flying on your T-shirt or hat? Is the community seeing support from you during its activities? Are they seeing a rainbow of happy, beautiful faces from your organization? If each of your members is modeling this behavior, getting volunteers to fill roles and getting members to attend your functions become much easier.

Businesses

How does your business create a crew-munity? How about company-sponsored lunches around the holidays and other special occasions? Does your business sponsor, or organize, after-hour sports? Are spouses and children invited to attend? One company Deb worked for had a big weekend holiday party for families, complete with Santa and elves, food, gift exchanges, and holiday music. Every year this event was always marked on the calendar way in advance. Year after year, the camaraderie at these events was discussed. Management became Santa and elves, and everyone had a role in the fun. Or what about a summer picnic for families in your community? You could have the highest-ranking community leader pass out trophies for performance in front of the families. Recognition is an especially great motivator and leads to better engagement, according to Gallup's Q^{12} Employee Engagement Survey, the most recognizable tool for employee engagement, introduced in Gallup's book *First, Break All the Rules*. It is a well-known and powerful tool for measuring engagement. According to Q^{12}, encouraging a "best friend at work" is also a way to build relationships, trust, and engagement. Again, Gallup's Q^{12} finds that those organizations that invest in relationships at work are more likely to be engaged. How about a company-sponsored mentor program for all employee levels, which provides frameworks for regulations, norms, and ethics? All associates could be paid to talk to their mentor for at least one hour a month. These conversations could be unstructured, but the primary objective would be to develop individuals, invest in them, and build relationships all across the company. Through this interaction a bond is formed and crew-munity begins. For example, Sodexo Corporation has an inclusion-inspired mentoring program that produces an incredible ROI. For every dollar spent on mentoring, nineteen dollars are returned. The point here is that inclusion can drive bottom-line results and Sodexo has proven it through its program.

Communities

Communities can be the easiest places to create an inclusive environment. There are no rules of engagement (businesses have those nasty productivity and metric requirements) and activities that please the community are always been encouraged. Try inexpensive activities such as a parade during certain holidays. Even neighborhoods can put together a parade or a softball game. Forest City, North Carolina, for instance, has many community events, the Christmas lighting event being the biggest. Every year, on Thanksgiving Day, thousands of lights that have been strung during the previous months are lit. There's hot chocolate, carriage rides, and even though it is late in the evening, shops and restaurants stay open for the event. The population of this town might only be about 8,000, but they know how to create a crew-munity. Another way to build your own crew-munity could be through potlucks or progressive dinners, which can also be fun. These dinners don't put the host or hostess on the spot for the whole meal. Neighbors show up for an appetizer at one house, go to another house for the main meal, and then to another for dessert. After-dinner drinks could even take neighbors to a fourth home. These inexpensive activities create crew-munity and the more activities there are, the more crew-munity is created.

DEEP DIVE

DEEP DIVE: SIX QUESTIONS TO EVALUATE YOUR CREW-MUNITY?

Creating a crew-munity takes shared social experiences, social interactions, shared missions, and accountability to each other. There are six critical questions to ask your organization or community to determine if you've set the right foundation for a crew-munity.

1. Does your organization have at least two or three activities annually where there are shared activities and families are welcome?

2. Are specific individuals recognized during these events?

3. Do these events showcase the best things about your organization? Is there something you want to showcase, such as an anchor product, a specific talent, or something that the crew-munity can rally around?

4. Is there conflict between social groups in your organization or in the case of community, between police and the community or some other public services in the community? Remember our discussion about something as benign as a driver's license office? Is yours making people who are new to the community feel welcome?

5. How does your organization handle personal space violations? Do you allow the team to work through them before leaders get involved?

6. What kind of submersion program to promote acceptance are you conducting in your business or community? Is there a way to get your team so engaged that they are laser-focused on the mission?

CHAPTER 4

EVERYONE MATTERS, IF THEY CONTRIBUTE: ALL OF US WILL ALWAYS BE BETTER THAN ONE OF US

Inclusion only works by educating people on understanding the things getting in the way of an inclusive environment. Diversity is the mix. Inclusion is making the mix work.

—Diversityinc.com

For many years, when it came to inclusion in the military, the elephant in the room was women. In 2010 women could assume roles on a submarine. I served on submarines prior to 2010, so I can only speak of my experiences then, but even though women were not full-time sailors on a submarine while I was serving, women were present, either to work on the submarine in port, or as part of a special mission.

When I think about the topic of women serving on submarines, one occasion always comes to mind. One day during our daily briefing, we were told about a mission that required a particular set of talents. A lieutenant was going to join us who was so special that she was one of one. We simply could not complete this mission without her unique talents. We were asked to make accommodations for her as she would be with us for an unknown period. Keep in mind that on the best of days we were cramped with no privacy, but we knew we had to provide special accommodation for the lieutenant, even if it were limited.

We thought it through carefully and decided to give her a bed in the general berthing room. We would ask everyone to wear boxers (a few of us slept naked), and we would give her a sign marked, "Woman on Board," so that when she used the officer shower or head, she could place it on the head door and have privacy.

We felt good about our decisions, which provided good accommodation without the risk of building resentment. With space and privacy so limited, going too far with accommodations might not be viewed positively, risking raising problems and part or all of the mission. However, we felt we had come up with a good plan and hoped the mission specialist would feel the same.

It turned out that the lieutenant asked for nothing more and was completely satisfied with what we came up with. With the task complete, we shifted our focus to the mission that she was such a critical component of and what we needed to do to complete it successfully. Nothing else changed and right before the lieutenant boarded, we announced she would be coming on board and was mission critical, as we would do for anyone. Word of mouth communicated the special accommodation arrangements. We were ready for the mission.

The lieutenant spent most of her time on that mission in the radio room, occasionally stopping by the mess deck for coffee and joining whoever was there. She was quiet and respectful and fit in remarkably well. It didn't occur to me until years later that, regardless of the differences, our focus on the mission and the role of each contributor kept us moving in the right direction. With the mission wrapped up successfully, the lieutenant was asked to join a debrief with several of the senior staff, including myself. I will never forget her poise as she described her experience. She said she felt very welcome on board, that the mission had been one of her longest on a submarine, and that she appreciated the accommodation. But what she appreciated most was that she really felt like one of the team. It was one of a long line of experiences that cemented my view that inclusion and mission were critical to moving away from differences and toward appreciation of strengths and contribution.

> **Regardless of the differences, our focus on the mission and the role of each contributor kept us moving in the right direction.**

When I shared this story with Deb, she said that in her business experience as a woman in a male world, such as when she worked with insurance agencies in the 1990s, acceptance and inclusion led to the highest level of engagement. Early on, she experienced sexual harassment and a glass ceiling that was hard to break, but as more women began to contribute, they bumped against this ceiling, taking on more and more critical roles. She was not surprised that being included and not being made to feel *different* could lead to an increased feeling of satisfaction in the mission itself. So, there you have it from another business expert: putting social groups together to solve a problem creates inclusion, and giving them time to socialize and share also creates openness.

EVERYONE MATTERS IF THEY CONTRIBUTE: USING STRENGTHS TO YOUR ADVANTAGE

I must admit that the navy was not focused on using strengths in any meaningful way, but it was a focus of mine. This was pretty much intuitive for me until I came to understand strengths, first from Gallup's book *First, Break All the Rules*, and then from Gallup's training certification program. I always thought if you can position people so that they are good or even great at something—what author Jim Collins, in his book *Good to Great,* calls "putting the right people in the right seat on the bus"—then you really have something. Jim Collins was the first significant businessperson and author, even prior to Gallup, to realize strengths are significant to engagement. As I rose in the naval ranks, my ability to influence things also increased, and I consistently positioned people for success, whether on the subs I was on or later at the training command where I was responsible for the successful training of over 2,000 members of all branches of military service.

> **If you focus people on what they love, or at least like a lot, you get improved engagement and it is significantly easier to build a true crew-munity.**

What does positioning people in their strengths have to do with diversity and inclusion? Ask yourself this: When people are unhappy or bored, are they more likely to pick on each other, disagree, or even bully? If you focus people on what they love, or at least like a lot, you get improved engagement and it is significantly easier to build a true crew-munity.

So how do strengths work? In their introduction to *Now Discover Your Strengths*, Marcus Buckingham and Donald Clifton talk about human beings' fixation with fault and failing and how this does nothing to improve overall performance. Our focus on studying and correcting faults to make people stronger has never proven to work. Remember, in the last chapter, I mentioned that the subs I served on were preoccupied with systemic failures so we could build better plans to avoid them? Studying human failures won't help to get the right people in the right seat and working in their strengths. Later, we will talk about the failure of processes, which is very different from focusing on human failure.

When it came to identifying people's strengths, I was lucky. Before we had tools to identify strengths, I used my instincts. I instinctively knew how to give people the job they could excel at. At that point, I had no idea that a tool (Strengthfinders) would be developed and I would work at the company that developed it: Gallup.

Getting people to use their talent reminds me of a story that I continue to tell in speeches and in my writing. It involves the positive change that one young man made to his character, a change that is still impacting the US Navy today. Unlike most new crew members, this young man, from the rough streets of Philadelphia, did not drop his prejudices or anything else when his feet hit the steel deck, and his attitude about all of us was quite clear: he knew it all and we were in his way. Despite this, he was charismatic and smart and had a few people on his side, enough to be promoted to the rank of seaman apprentice. It was rare for someone to be promoted and still cause problems. Generally, those crew members flunked out of the navy.

And as different as we were, this young man, an African American from Philadelphia, and I, a Caucasian from New York, had a lot in common. There were qualities in him that I recognized in myself: confidence, a desire to be successful, and a load of moxie. He picked fights repeatedly and to say he had an attitude was to completely underestimate his impact on the boat. He caused high tension every time he entered a room. His mentor—what submariners call a sea daddy—tried working with him, coaching him and prepping him for watch duty, but he pushed back at everything. His idea of solving a problem was, first, with his fists.

One day, at wits end, the chief came to me. To really understand how unusual this was, you have to remember the submarine culture. Problems were solved at the lowest possible level. Focus was on the mission and chiefs did not get into the day-to-day conflicts of any sailor. But this young man was different. He did not play by any rules but his own. He could have quickly been separated from the navy, but there was something about him: he had promise. So the first thing I did after the chief filled me in on the details—uncooperative, belligerent, refusing to study for watch—was to have a crucial conversation with the young man.

The expression "swear like a sailor" has a bit more than a kernel of truth to it, and that truth was not absent from my crucial conversation that day. I would not say that, outside the navy, military, or submarine services, swearing is a good way to communicate, but it was how we did it. Volume, foul language, and very specific language about the problem came to that young man from about five inches in front of his face. If my memory is correct, I told him that we were a lot alike, but I was willing to work hard to become good at what I did, while he refused to even put any effort into himself, which left him just a punk without a skill. In response, he squared his shoulders, and I thought for the first time in my career that I was going to get punched. The rage showed on his face, but then it left. "I don't want to be a punk," he said. "I want to be good at what I do. I want to be the best assistant navigator like you are, Senior Chief."

I told him I was happy to hear that, but he needed to get on track quickly or he was going to get tossed out of the navy.

I won't say it was perfect after that day. That young man had many years of survival skills and scars to overcome. In fact, a little while after we had "the talk," he got into an argument with the chief cook, who had taken the young man's hat after he had left it in the mess deck. Just in time, I caught both of them screaming at each other. Although the chief cook was a big dude, my young seaman probably would have beaten him senseless. I gave the young man his hat and sent him on his way.

Thankfully, that was the last big incident, because after that, the young man qualified for watch and we immediately saw him start to contribute in ways that made a real difference. He became a member of the team, and not only did he straighten out but he also ended up having a remarkable career with the navy. He served ten years as a quartermaster—my role, just as he had wanted—and then went to college, where he was commissioned. He eventually became a commanding officer. Finding value, gaining expertise, and qualifying all contributed to a challenging young seaman's transition to a successful career in the navy.

From my vantage point of both serving on submarines and later working for my consulting company, I've found that focusing on strengths and not differences, such as skin color or sexual orientation, helps deliver inclusive teams. If we were to spend more time appreciating strengths and worrying less about failure in people, we'd have stronger teams and get better results. Gallup's Q^{12} Employee Engagement Survey question proves this when it asks, "At work, do you have the opportunity to do what you do best every day?" According to Gallup, when employees answer yes, their company is 50 percent more likely to have lower turnover, while 38 percent of employees are more likely to work in more productive business units, and 44 percent are more likely to work in business units with higher satisfaction scores.

When Deb and I were client and consultant, we shared the same viewpoint about the need for strengths in leadership and organization. We had lively discussions long before we were a couple or had a formal understanding of strengths. We both talked about the number-one benefit of strength-based organizations as an important step to developing inclusive teams.

THE POWER OF A STRENGTH-BASED TEAM

The best example I can give of a strength-based team was the one involved with the first SEAL delivery vehicle on my fourth submarine, the USS *L. Mendel Rivers,* during my second tour on her. This team was not built from rank or title but from talent and expertise. We didn't know how to do anything: launch the vehicle, get it to float—we knew nothing. All the computations from the naval design procedures turned out to not work. We had to start with a clean sheet of paper, but each person brought a talent and expertise to this project that was necessary. With the right talent, within a week, we completely rewrote the procedure. We could launch and recover the SEAL delivery vehicle in any weather. If we had been chosen according to rank, it might never have worked. That's how powerful everyone contributing in their own way can be.

TACTICAL READINESS: FOUR QUESTIONS TO IDENTIFY STRENGTHS

Gallup defines strength as consistent, near-perfect performance. Can you think of something you do that, almost every time, you do nearly perfectly? Gallup maintains that if you have a strength, you must have it consistently. People who can sing one song well on the TV show *The Voice* will not make the finals. They will be just a one-hit wonder much admired for that one song. So how do you or your team determine what your strengths are? Let's face it, if we all work in our strengths, there is a synergy that goes beyond the individual. If you look close enough at what your team gravitates to, you'll find that Bob loves reports and is consistently good at them, Sally loves to lead people and is always volunteering to do the onboarding of new employees, and Mike loves to manage. If there's a call with senior management, Mike is going to volunteer to handle it. As I said, I like public speaking and

John's Story: Finding My Own Strength

I mentioned earlier that I found a general lack of awareness of strengths during my naval service, but there were exceptions. As a senior chief, I was asked to attend the Senior Enlisted Academy. This was unusual because, generally, only master chiefs were invited to attend. I was very articulate, outspoken, and a good public speaker, and had somehow been identified as the prototype enlisted crew member in the new navy. The days of the gruff and grumbling senior chief were gone. To be honest, I do not know what this new navy candidate looks like today, so my view is a snapshot in time. I attended the academy in Newport, Rhode Island, with forty master chiefs. They outranked me and had more years in service, and years on Earth. I have always looked young for my age, and I did not look my age of thirty-eight years. Despite that fact, I fit in very well, and we prepared for one of us to speak directly to the undersecretary of the navy on a topic we all chose. As we all worked together on the topic and the speaking points, it became clear to the others that although I was the youngest and held the lowest rank, I was the right person to address the undersecretary. I prepared for the speech and delivered it with passion. It was evident to everyone, including me, that this was something I loved. From that day forward, if there were a speech or a public message to be delivered, I would be one of the top choices. Thank you, navy.

people, and anything that can get me to work with either. Thank goodness I have always been able to use my gifts.

Right now, there are four questions you can ask yourself and your team to help you identify your strengths:

1. When it comes to your perceived strength, can you get to almost perfect performance with practice? If the answer is no, then it's likely not a strength.

2. Do you enjoy the activity as whole? If I am singing on *The Voice* and I really enjoy singing that one song, but I feel great panic and discomfort when asked to sing something else, that likely means that singing is not my strength.

3. What are your other talents? I found that mine are related to my ability to speak, such as writing and coaching. How often have you put the wrong butt in the wrong seat and gotten a poor result? Learning how to help or coach others and place and develop them in the appropriate roles is a very important skill and lays the foundation for an inclusive team.

4. How will you coach others to employ their strengths? How will you refer to talent and skills? How will you encourage and motivate someone to perfect a talent? If you are leading people and struggling with developing an inclusive team, you need language to help you develop their individual talents into strengths. For example, an employer interviewing for a programmer position rejects a candidate because the team has determined that the candidate is not a great communicator. Another example would be a panel interview of a quiet introvert who would be spending time on financial spreadsheets. That person

would likely be very intimidated by a million questions asked by all the panel members, so a panel interview might not be the best approach.

Are you helping your team see the relevant talents needed for the job and helping them focus on them? If your company is still stuck in the 1980s, it's time for an update. Look for the skills and talent you need in a role and interview primarily for those skills and talent. Encourage your teams to look not just at experience but also at talents that are relevant to the job. A panel interview for communications skills doesn't make sense for a position in which the employee spends 80 percent of the time on programming. What talents should you be hiring for? What are the best strengths for each seat in your organization's bus?

BE THE BEST YOU CAN BE

Working with strengths is more than just a one-time event. Getting good at something takes practice and identifying the thing you are good at is critical. Eventually, with

> For me, spending hours and hours getting better at spreadsheets is not going to be helpful when I love to talk to people. Instead, I should focus on being the best communicator I can possibly be.

everyone focused on strengths, engagement goes up and real change happens in the culture. In tying back to the notion of preoccupation with failure, it is human nature to want to fix things, but a strength-focused approach is just the opposite. For me, spending hours and hours getting better at spreadsheets is not going to be helpful when I love to talk to people. Instead, I should focus on being the best communicator I can possibly be.

We use this approach with products we work on and in evaluating and developing our employees. What employees want to be appreciated simply because they are male, female, or gay? People want to be appreciated for their strengths and contribution. We cannot build strong and diverse teams if we don't allow and encourage people to be the best they can be. We might be lucky enough to create diversity by this means, but if we spend our time trying to fix people instead of focusing on talents and skills, what are the chances that we are getting the best results for our effort? I can say this with absolute confidence: when I used my gift for identifying and developing strengths on a team, loyalty to, and focus on, the missions were always maintained, whether it was in the Atlantic fighting the bad guys, or increasing sales with my sales team at Media General. Those relationships we built in the navy on subs are still alive today. We do not see each other as much as we used to, but lively conversations about the mission and our relationship with each other has not lost its glow even after all these years. None of us slipped back into bias and prejudice against each other. We maintain focus on the mission even now.

> **We cannot build strong and diverse teams if we don't allow and encourage people to be the best they can be.**

LEADING WITH YOUR TEAM

A strength-based approach to leadership helped me deliver inclusion with my navy crew and my Media General teams. Strength-based leadership is critical to diversity and inclusion—an entire book can be devoted to it—but I will just touch on it here. Strength-based leadership uses the TEAM approach:

T is for talent. Talent needs to be diverse, with the individual's passion identified and focused by the leader. A common development language for the coach and the individual also needs to be agreed upon.

E is for engagement. Once people are focused on what they are good at, you have the start of an engaged team. All team members focusing on what they love creates engagement.

A is for aim. Outcomes need to be clear and focused on the M (mission). What outcome are you expecting from this engaged team? The US Navy, Media General, and the cross-divisional company that Deb managed all had very clear outcomes.

M is for mission. Talent, engagement, and outcome need to be mission focused. Once the right talent is identified, the focus is on completing the mission.

If you are struggling to get the best from your diverse team and you have followed The System's steps of inclusion, then strength-based leadership might be what's lacking. It is very likely you have the right butts in the wrong seats. Build a team with this strength-based TEAM approach to inclusion!

QUALIFICATION: MAKING EVERYONE MATTER

On submarines, qualifications never end: Think continuous professional development, regardless of how senior you are. When your feet hit the steel deck for the first time, you only had a moment or two to take a look around before you were reminded of the mission and that there was work to do. The most important thing a new sailor on a submarine needs to do is qualify for watch, which can be downright brutal. I worked with a senior chief who wouldn't acknowledge the existence of a new sailor until he qualified. He would walk around that sailor, ignore him, and pretend he didn't exist. I believe he really didn't think he did exist until he qualified.

When I served with the US Navy, the pressure to qualify for watch was incredible, but the support to do so was equally impressive. Each new sailor was provided a sea daddy, who pushed, motivated, and answered questions about the qualification process. A sea daddy's responsibility was so important that if the new sailor didn't qualify in a timely manner, both the sea daddy and the sailor heard from the crew. It was not unheard of for an unsuccessful sea daddy to also get a study time assignment.

The pressure on the sailor and the sea daddy is incredible and it's hard to duplicate in any other environment. It's an extreme level of accountability, but accountability, whether it's in a community, business, or faith organization, is critical to inclusion. This pressure on the new sailor and the sea daddy is so consistent and pervasive that it becomes a norm. No one would consider letting up on this expectation to qualify because to do so puts everyone at risk.

TACTICAL READINESS: EVERYONE MATTERS IF THEY CONTRIBUTE—QUESTIONS FOR BUSINESSES, FAITH ORGANIZATIONS AND COMMUNITIES

Faith Organizations

How does your faith organization *qualify* or make sure everyone contributes so that everyone is valued? Are individuals taught about the values of the church? Are there processes that need to be learned for each volunteer task? Do you need to qualify for each role, volunteer or not? It is almost counterintuitive to make people try out for a volunteer role, but the reality is that volunteerism is appreciated more by both the administrators and the volunteers if qualifying for the activity has meaning. Are the norms of contributing to the organization and becoming familiar with its operations so strong that they are incorporated into everyone? If so, absenteeism is likely infrequent and a long line of applicants are waiting to participate. An even more unusual notion is to seek key roles outside your organization. A Facebook post such as "Church seeking guitarist to play with choir on Sundays" might be just what someone is looking for. If you want to develop an engaged diverse faith organization, social media, including Twitter and Instagram, offer a way to appeal to a wide variety of talents and backgrounds. Show your shining faces on Facebook and see who shows up at your next service, and, maybe, this will inspire the needed talent or skill you're looking for. Making sure everyone has a role and the organization is diverse leads to a new level of inclusion. It also means your church's norms are so strong everyone contributes whenever possible.

Businesses

Business is probably the easiest of the three organizational entities in which to build a culture where everyone contributes something important, because a high level of accountability is critical to ensuring every associate *qualifies for submarine watch*. If new employees do the minimum needed for their job, sustained engagement will not occur. Putting pressure on employees is easy, but keeping them engaged with all the pressure is not. Instead, you should be communicating clear expectations, providing training, and encouraging norms so strong that inclusion is the only option. Think about where you work today or where you've worked in the past. Was there an issue because the environment was cliquey? Perhaps the boss liked certain people and not others, and no one could figure out why. What if the most popular people were those who contributed to fighting the submarine? What if they were sea daddies to new associates, the trainers who could fix the printer, who knew code, or who had specific computer skills they shared with others, or they had some other formal or informal role that made the business so productive, so mission focused, and inclusive that everyone wanted to be a part of it? And yes, a business like this can be efficient. All of us will always be faster and better than one of us if we work together.

Communities

A lot has been written about the importance of civic duty. Peter Drucker, in his book *Management Challenges for the 21st Century*, believes civic duty is giving to the community in pursuit of one's own interest or activity. John Gardner, in his book *On Leadership*, argues that a social system in which people can pursue their respective views of common good is what makes that system livable and workable for all. Both of those statements take a position on the value of everyone to the common good of the community. How does one determine what people can contribute to the common good? Let's use the analogy of the submarine again as a microcosm of communities. In my submarine experience, sea daddies were good at mentoring new sailors; they were highly skilled at what they did and had a way of applying pressure to a new sailor without breaking him. Every individual in a community has something to offer if you look below the surface. Is someone in your community a good organizer? Are that person's neighborhood parties the best: the food is excellent, the entertainment perfect, the mix of attendees exactly right? What if this person were to be tapped to organize some important community initiative? Once an attempt is made to tap community members according to their strengths, momentum builds and volunteerism goes up. This is only one example of civic duty. There are as many examples of tapping people according to their strengths as there are people. Get to know individuals in your community, identify their strengths, and tap them to do something important.

DEEP DIVE

SIX QUESTIONS TO EVALUATE YOUR TEAM MEMBERS' CONTRIBUTIONS

How is your organization getting everyone to contribute?

1. Are the participants at critical meetings always the same people? If the answer is yes, it is likely you are not tapping into many who could contribute.

2. When solving problems, are you asking who is in charge, or who is best at fixing the issue? If the answer is who is in charge, you are focused too much on hierarchy and not on talent-based inclusion.

3. If you are in a leadership role, can you quickly name the one or two things the people who report to you *love* to do? If not, find out today.

4. How does your organization qualify new team members?

5. Are the right people in the right seats?

6. Are you hiring the right people, and when they are fully trained, are you holding them accountable for results?

CHAPTER 5

OMBUDSMEN: THE SQUARE KNOTS IN THE SUBMARINE WORLD

A square knot joins pieces of line together in such a way that they are tightly bound but can easily be separated if needed. This is something that an ombudsman does perfectly and it is why every organization needs at least one. Mentoring, supporting, and liaison were all critical functions when I served on a submarine. The ombudsman

> **The ombudsman had a unique role that encompassed a little, or a lot, of mentoring, supporting, and liaising with the families back home.**

had a unique role that encompassed a little, or a lot, of mentoring, supporting, and liaising with the families back home. This role was so critical to keeping the families, command, and crew operating that it came with training and was considered a role with status. It was also a formal role with formal status, and it was so important to crewmunity, to the families of deploying crew, and to the command that it was part of The System. The other roles in this chapter are important but do not make it to The System. Ombudsmen are the square knots that tie The System together.

In the US Navy, ombudsman volunteers are generally the spouses of the highest-ranking enlisted submariner in the command. They are the communication link between the commanding officer and the family members. They help families get what they need, especially during deployment. Remember how we submariners saw ourselves as a little village and when we deployed, the little village stayed intact? Well, the ombudsman is partly responsible for this little village. In the early years, this volunteer role could entail serving as a chauffeur, holding the hand of the sick loved one of a deploying crew member, or playing counselor for a couple's marital problems before they became an issue for the command. In recent years, the role has evolved to serving as the communication link between deploying spouses and their family, as the link to command and referral services, and even as a means of helping people work through governmental red tape. As I researched online the role of ombudsmen today, over and over I saw blogs and articles on their value. They not only help to eliminate red tape with the government, but they also give referrals to doctors, dentists, home repairers, plumbers— whatever service is required—and they offer an ear when needed. They are also privy to nonconfidential orders that family members are not privy to and can help with forwarding critical family messages to deploying crews.

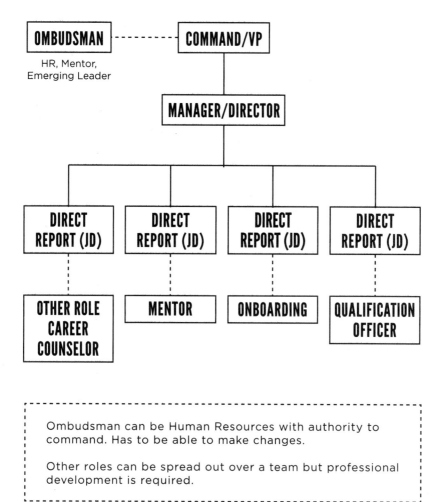

```
┌──────────────┐           ┌──────────────┐
│  OMBUDSMAN   │---------- │  COMMAND/VP  │
└──────────────┘           └──────────────┘
  HR, Mentor,
  Emerging Leader
```

Ombudsman can be Human Resources with authority to command. Has to be able to make changes.

Other roles can be spread out over a team but professional development is required.

I still recall an ombudsman helping me untangle a confusing situation. I was the re-fit coordinator for an extremely intense three-month maintenance period. When you were on the re-fit team, you weren't supposed to have any additional responsibility, but on this mission, I received word from the chief of the boat that a machinist mate on my team was working two jobs. He had his divisional duties and he had his re-fit duties. He had been doing double duty for two weeks, likely working twenty hours a day, and hadn't made it home. This surfaced because the wife of the missing machinist called the ombudsman, who called the chief of the boat, who called me. It was not uncommon for someone to absorb the workload—we all did—and if it had not been for the ombudsman, this confusion would not have surfaced. The machinist wasn't to blame; he was doing what he had been told to do.

Deb recalls her long hours working for a brand-new company in Houston, Texas. For several months, she and many others had been working sixteen to eighteen hours a day, seven days a week, to prepare for a market opening that could not be missed. One Sunday night as she drove home, she missed her exit and found herself in completely unfamiliar territory. She was simultaneously asleep and awake at the wheel, and much to her surprise, it took her forty-five minutes to get back to her exit. She was so tired that her ability to focus was gone. She believes if ombudsmen were to have direct access to authorities and were empowered to intervene, they could resolve many issues, including helping a very overworked team in Houston.

There are other critical roles on a submarine that are filled by volunteers: literally, people with more than full-time jobs who step up to support the full needs of the sailors. Three of those roles are career counselors, qualification officers, and mentors.

CAREER COUNSELORS

On a submarine, these individuals always have a primary job, such as assistant navigator, in addition to being a career counselor. They are so important that they have an actual navy rating, a full-time job. On a submarine, because we all wear many hats, this is a major collateral duty. Some of the duties include overall responsibility for the command's career development programs, conducting interviews, and providing command assistance. They are responsible for career development and retention and posting the names of those who are up for promotion. They talk to individual crew members about dream sheets (where they might want to go on their next assignment) and provide all the study material for career advancement. It's a big job and 100 percent voluntary on a submarine. If you don't care about people, their careers, and their engagement, this wouldn't be the job for you. Career counselors are completely focused on crew members' careers, which helps to keep the crew engaged. This is an example of the differences between submarines and surface ships. If a fire breaks out on a surface ship, the crew waits for the fire-fighting experts to arrive. On a sub, however, everyone fights a fire and everyone has multiple roles. This helps build an inclusive environment. What would it be like if your organization had someone completely focused on careers? Do you think turnover could be reduced and do you think you'd have better engagement?

QUALIFICATION OFFICER

I am sure all branches of the US Navy, as well as other branches of the US military, are proud of their warfare qualifications, but I speak of submarines. Since the first one was launched, submarine qualification has been required. Failing to do so within the time limits means permanent removal from the submarine force. Every single crew member understands how critical this is and looks to the qualification officer for support and to make sure qualification is achieved on time. Getting those dolphins on his chest is the most inclusive thing any crew member can do. I still wear my dolphins when I speak publicly. On submarines, you are not part of the crew until you are qualified. I remember that on one boat, they had a "non-qual hat" versus a "qualified hat" to distinguish the two. The non-qual had literally had only the boat name and hull number, no dolphins. To contrast this, for my brothers and sisters on surface ships, qualification was optional until 2010, something that was unimaginable to a submariner.

The qualification officer is responsible for qualifying on submarines and for watch. Regardless of whether sailors have already been qualified on the same class of submarine, they need to qualify again. The good news was that it is much easier the second time around. In submarine school, a new crew member must learn all the major systems. This is an eight-week, extremely academic exercise. Before new sailors set foot on a submarine, they are already familiar with all the major systems. The qualification officer takes them from a general understanding to a specific understanding of all systems, significant valves, compartments, and every piece of damage control equipment on their specific submarine. Much of the crew supported the qualification officer. As experts in the various systems, they would provide check-outs to the crew member to ensure a sufficient level of knowledge. Submarine qualification is the most significant event in a submariner's career.

MENTORS

Another key component found in various forms is the mentor/mentee relationship. Along with the more formal roles of the positions discussed above, the mentor can provide great guidance in helping the sailor understand norms and how to better self-regulate.

Norms and regulations exist in business and are broken frequently. Many companies have an ethics department, corporate lawyers, and ethics training, but from a practical standpoint, ethics and norms in most companies are not transparent until they are broken. Transparency is particularly important in businesses where associate engagement drives turnover and bottom-line results. Additionally, mentor programs can provide frameworks for regulations, norms, and ethics. Mentor programs exist today, but for the most part, they aren't all that well done. As a mentee, Deb found that a lot of her mentoring experiences have been a waste of time. When she was a mentor, she tried to be everything she had hoped her own mentor would be, but she received little formal training. Problems arise because mentors don't understand how to mentor properly or are not available. What if mentors were to understand the norms and how to navigate the organization, and were to receive some training in mentoring? What if a mentor were to become as important as a sea daddy is when getting a sailor to qualify is mission critical? A mentor should have access to an ombudsman if there are ethics violations, bullying, or any other behavior destructive to the business's mission. Mentors should be the organization's self-regulation and norm safety net.

TACTICAL READINESS: OMBUDSMEN
QUESTIONS FOR BUSINESSES, FAITH ORGANIZATIONS AND COMMUNITIES

Faith Organizations

While the role of ombudsman is often played by the leader of the organization or that person's spouse, the truly important thing to consider is this volunteer's role. In a faith organization, this person could be responsible for providing information on treatment centers, doctors, and local hospitals, and for coordinating prayer lines for the ill, and similar services. He or she might also be the liaison for families in need, directing them to community services such as food pantries, the Red Cross, or Salvation Army. This volunteer might also be privy to organizational processes, rules, or structures that affect individual members and be able to advise on them. The role could be voluntary but should also be so important that it becomes the backbone of the faith community. Just as the ombudsman needs training, this volunteer needs training on what is expected, and how to respond if situations go beyond his or her skill or comfort level.

Businesses

The role of an ombudsman in business is often compensated and given the title of human resource generalist. HR staff are very important to an organization, but let's face it, they know how things are supposed to work and not necessarily how they really do. They also represent the business's interests, not necessarily the interests of the associates. What if each business unit had an ombudsman who helped communicate directly with the *command?* What if they were the people who communicated pay equity issues, morale and engagement issues, and other problems that prevent the business from being all it could be? These individuals would have access to executives who could solve associate problems before they became a problem for the business. Such ombudsmen would not be compensated for filtering the message or handling the situation as some HR professionals might be. They would be rewarded for helping to resolve issues or bring up matters that are causing problems, or likely to cause problems, in the business. They would have the power to communicate this information to the highest level of leadership. Once something is so serious that its effects can be measured, the problem becomes that much more difficult to resolve, and once ingrained, it becomes a cultural issue with a significantly higher cost of resolution. Needless to say, the business ombudsman must have the emotional intelligence necessary to handle this very critical role.

Communities

The ombudsman in the community must know how to have access to city officials, decision makers, services, and other community resources. Unless ombudsmen are volunteers, getting a sufficient number of them might be difficult. In general, the community ombudsman must have a special knack for cutting through red tape. For example, if you need a construction permit and can't find the right party to get it, you should be able to consult an ombudsman, who can place a call and open the right doors to get things done. For newcomers to the community, this could make the difference between a very unpleasant experience and one that opens doors to hassle-free living. And what if there were self-regulation? What if the ombudsman were the first to be told about a rogue cop before that cop's behavior became a widespread problem? What if the ombudsman were the first to learn that a public official was involved in inappropriate behavior? The community ombudsman would need to be strong, possess emotional intelligence, understand community governance inside and out, and have credibility with those responsible for stopping bad behavior. The position could be compensated, or not, but a volunteer is likely to take an unbiased approach, which is very appealing.

Deb and I found through our research that many social services organizations have ombudsmen, such as those who assist the elderly or the handicapped, and they are not uncommon in larger communities. This prompted me to look deeper into ombudsman positions around the country. I found that they were most often compensated, which might appeal to those with the education, experience, and desire to help the elderly, or help provide fair housing, or had an interest in helping the disabled. It was encouraging to see that a role critical to improving communication in the military could also provide value in communities. With this key role in place, communities could put the other pieces of The System together to drive inclusion.

DEEP DIVE

DEEP DIVE: WHO IS YOUR OMBUDSMAN, CAREER OFFICER, OR QUALIFICATION OFFICER?

Mentoring, support and liaising are critical to The System and later, we will discuss the impact on engagement. Who is your ombudsman, career officer, or qualification officer, and how seriously does that person take the role? Any community or faith organization would benefit from someone focused on growth and development, as well the ombudsman's role as liaison and communication specialist.

1. Who is responsible for career development in your organization? Are there many such people, as on a submarine, or is there no one?

2. Who makes sure there is a square knot in the critical functions of a command? Is the HR staff member, with an already full workload, also responsible for career development, promotion, and training?

3. Who has command's ear and helps to prevent dissatisfaction from leading to engagement issues?

4. How helpful would it be if your church, business, or community had an ombudsman?

CHAPTER 6

FOCUS ON THE MISSION: WHY MISSION AND PURPOSE ARE CRITICAL TO SUCCESS

F ocusing on the mission isn't the last step in The System because it is least important. In fact, it is the *most important* step, but it cannot be achieved without steps one through four. You need a structure to support the mission and the steps of *check-in, crew-munity, everyone contributes,* and *appointing an Ombudsman* are all necessary for the mission to be successful. And yes, infrastructure and processes are all necessary to run the faith organization, business, or community. However, for the success of all participants, there needs to be more: a system.

Inclusion does not happen accidentally, as I had thought it did all those years ago. It happens with a strategy that, if repeated consistently, results in norms so strong that inclusion is the result. So how critical is defining the mission? Defining the mission keeps the team driving toward a goal. With a strong mission, personal differences get worked out quickly so the mission isn't compromised. Remember the story of the female lieutenant who was mission critical because of her special talent? The team quickly responded to her accommodation needs, overcame the prevalent superstition that women on board brought bad luck, and included the lieutenant in the planning and the daily activities of the boat, all because the mission was well defined with clear deliverables and deadlines. The mission was accomplished successfully, but perhaps equally important, it occurred without incident and with full inclusion of the needed personnel.

Defining the mission might be a quarterly exercise or a daily reminder of what the purpose of the team is, or what the contribution of each team member is. For instance, one mission I was on was so critical and so confidential that I can't discuss the details, but I can share this: all crew members knew their unique role in this mission, and those roles were based on individuals' unique talents to achieve the mission. Every day, there was a short brief on goals and accomplishments, all normal duties were rotated between crew members to improve focus, and the mission was so clear that no one was confused about what he was there to do. The mission created a synergy that caused everyone to step up and do more than his fair share. Communicating the mission and focusing kept the team energized and created the highest levels of participation.

Deb speaks of the difficulties she experienced when she worked in a division of a large company where sales were low and productivity was off the mark. The division was dependent on government legislation to drive sales and it appeared that the legislation would be disappearing, and soon. It was a transitional period, with the future unknown. Morale was low and focus on the mission was murky. Instead of allowing that situation to get him down, however, the senior vice president of Deb's division brought the leaders together, redefined the mission and goals, motivated the group, and sent them back out to accomplish the new mission. Deb always speaks of this leader as one who was so intuitive and innovative that he could respond to just about any change in business and adapt to achieve the mission. He taught her a tremendous amount about leadership and mission.

A business mission statement that is good and clear enough to be in place for a year or two might take one page. Strategy and tactics may change with new obstacles or new goals, but the mission stays the same. When I served on submarines, we used a four-step structure for achieving the mission, which, in turn, led to inclusion, along with the other pieces of The System:

FOUR STEPS FOR ACHIEVING THE MISSION

1. **Acceptance:** Acknowledge and welcome new people, ideas, and differences into your environment because every mission is different. On the submarine, acceptance didn't happen easily, but that had nothing to do with outward differences. Acceptance happened when someone was contributing to the mission, such as taking watch. If they didn't contribute to watch, which might be the *only* mission that day, it became a very tough environment indeed. When a new sailor hit the steel deck for the first time, tolerance was expected from the new sailor and the crew, as he worked at whatever needed to be done. Over

time, he needed to qualify for watch and once he qualified for watch and had his dolphins, he gained complete acceptance. Acceptance of the completely foreign world of life on a submarine took a while, but submersion into that world was critical.

2. **Embrace what you can't change because missions are orders:** When I was still a very junior petty officer on a sub, I somehow wound up with a bunk that only I slept in. I know that might not seem like a big deal, but remember the hot rack? I didn't spend a lot of time dwelling on it, but I never liked sharing a bunk with another dude. However, the free bunk had two issues: first, it was hard to get into because it was right under a high-pressure valve, and second, if that valve had failed, I would have died instantly.

    I took the bunk. I didn't worry about the valve bursting, because I knew I would die instantly. To me, this was a perfect example of choosing to focus only on the things you can control. I didn't tolerate those things I couldn't change; I embraced them for what they were. What mattered most to me was sleeping in my own bunk, not sleeping next to a pressure valve I would never even have known had failed. In the business world, personal space may take the form of having a private office, your own printer, or a desk next to a window. Decide what's important to you and what to focus on, and move on if it doesn't matter. If anything interferes with the mission, however, speak up.

    On a sub, a lot has to be embraced. Sleeping in a hot rack, the smell, work-outs in the engine room, and just keeping the noise down were all conditions we had to do more than tolerate; we had to embrace them.

Embracing the foul smell of submarine air instead of just temporarily tolerating it, for instance, was critical. To this day, bad smells really don't bother me that much because I not only built up a tolerance for them; I accepted them as a norm. In fact, one of my freshest memories (no pun intended) is pulling into port and opening the hatch. Fresh air poured in, but to us, it was beyond awful. New sailors would often say, "What is that foul odor?" It was fresh air. We had gotten so used to our own stink that fresh air had become the bad smell. To me, that is one of the clearest expressions of embracing the situation and moving beyond tolerance.

3. **Steady state:** You know you've moved past all the other phases when you are not thinking of tolerance, you've embraced the world around you with little reservation, you've accepted healthy conflict, and you are ignoring the little things and looking forward to the day.

    The term *steady state* has relevance in many fields, including thermodynamics and economics. When a system is in a steady state, it will remain relatively unchanged in the future. When I observed that regardless of the boat I was on, the crew, or their experience, The System of inclusion remained unchanged, I realized it could be repeated. And you don't need to be in the navy or on a submarine to duplicate the effect. In the business world, Deb's experience with systems is that once a solid system is in place, the result can be duplicated. In fact, employees get so ingrained in a system that *kaizen* (continuous improvement) must occur to maintain efficiency.

4. **Readiness, the state of being fully prepared for something:** When I think of readiness, I think of Captain Billings, not quite his name, but that's not important to the story. He was a brute of a man, over six feet tall, which, on a submarine, means you need to round your shoulders and duck your head constantly. His barrel chest could fill a walkway and his forearms were like ropes. Everyone was intimidated by him, including his XO. Captain Billings was old-school navy, tough without a gentle bone in his body, but he was *our* captain. He was *the* one we wanted to go to war with. He could take a brand-new crew and in a very short time turn them into warriors. We could go from tolerance to steady state to the highest readiness state in a short time and be as prepared as any group of warriors can be.

When we fought the submarine with Captain Billings, we all had a swagger. He was tough and smart, and had one of the best minds for strategy in the submarine navy. We were also on a nuclear submarine, a fast attack that had a crew with a reputation for quality, toughness, and readiness. Quite frankly, we were bad asses and we knew it. Everyone was focused on the mission and we were all working together to deliver it.

Readiness means you are prepared for the unexpected. If the best your organization can do is maintain a steady state, you will not be prepared for change, and from a diversity and inclusion perspective, you will not be responding consistently to changes at work or in a community.

This is what is happening in police forces around the country. Their training and recruitment is focused on skills and getting to a steady state, but when something truly unexpected comes along, they are not prepared to move to readiness quickly enough. If the organization does not have strong norms that allow the teams to monitor each other, it may be subject to random and destructive actions.

The Genesis Group, a consulting company I started, did a lot of coaching and training in police officer training programs around the country, and I always felt that if the training were expanded to include readiness as well as establishing strong norms, then they would be better prepared for those situations that are driving a wedge between police officers and the community today. On the submarine, pressure from the team itself created strong norms, so strong, in fact, that adverse behavior was limited and inclusion was the result. That kind of self-monitoring cannot be replaced with rules or laws.

A culture of readiness is not an easy one to build. Steady state is where most organizations want to be. As I researched the topic of readiness, there were many articles that focused on the need for *readiness for change,* which is what readiness is about. Steady state, as we discussed, is a status that remains unchanged, while readiness is the opposite: being prepared for change. And the reality is that the pace of change has accelerated. The Internet, travel, and global economic treaties leading to globalization in general have sped it up. Sociologists talk about anomie, or a state of normlessness, contributing to the increasing rate of violent crimes and murders. Without norms, there will be more and more violence around the world. Creating readiness helps society, communities, and businesses shift toward clearly defined norms, which anchor (a little nautical reference there, but completely fitting!) people to their communities, faith organizations, and businesses. Establishing clear norms in multiple scenarios in multiple communities, in my opinion, wins back peace in our communities and creates inclusion.

TACTICAL READINESS: FOUR CRITICAL STEPS TO READINESS

With years of business experience between the two of us, Deb and I believe there are four critical steps to readiness:

1. **Definition of success: identifying the result of the readiness state in advance.** The mission might be to respond to unexpected change. Let's say the mission is about handling the unexpected change of a fire in your office building. The procedure regulations need to identify the specific emergency, and the exits and leaders identified in advance. What would constitute the success of the mission must also be defined. Would it be successful when all employees have left the building? On the submarine, readiness for unexpected change such as a fire, nuclear power issue, or radiation problem is constantly top of mind. Drills, procedures, and discussion keep readiness for these events relevant and current. Success for us mariners was always that the submarine continued moving, providing air and water, with no, or few, casualties. Getting home was in there too, but keeping the sub operational was clearly the number-one priority.

2. **Identify someone whose neck is on the line if the desired result is not achieved.** A few years back, Deb

was responsible for a program that had great revenue potential and even greater visibility if it were to fail. She built the program with team members spanning a very large company population and presenting cross-divisional challenges. This effort not only encompassed the project but also a readiness plan, all of which needed to be built in thirty days. It was successfully launched, made the organization $75 million over eighteen months, and was the first cross-divisional effort and success of its kind. When I asked her what the key to this success was, she said it was having a solid readiness plan and one throat to choke: hers.

Once the owner of a result has been correctly identified, it is easier to cascade change throughout the organization and drive the change faster. This demonstrates the importance of accountability but also shows the value of positive role modeling and leadership. Later in this book we will discuss the importance of drilling, known as experiential training, for successful readiness preparation, as well as the criticality of leadership.

3. **Identify team members to communicate the plan, the training, and the desired outcome.** These individuals must be advocates and strong leader communicators. When I served on subs, the chiefs owned the result, but the crew carried out the mission. Each person was significant and each had a clear role. In her experience with the cross-divisional project, Deb found choosing the right people to communicate the message and to own the result was key to the success of her project. Each division had a

spokesperson who was held accountable to that division. If someone who was not on board with the project blocked the outcome, Deb had crucial conversations and went even further if necessary.

4. **Cultural transformation: the new culture must be described and the new behaviors integrated in daily activities to drive change.** For us submariners, drills, norms, and activities quickly pushed organizational change. A state of readiness is not the right term here; it was a matter of life and death. And each individual contributor also needed to be responsible for delivering this transformation. In the cross-divisional project that Deb worked on, clear objectives were assigned to each divisional leader and clear revenue goals outlined. Deb was responsible for the project overall, but each individual leader also had his or her area of accountability. Deb and her peers held each person accountable and if there was a failure at any step along the way, it was quickly addressed. They held meetings to review the progress of each step, what we submariners call drilling. When I served on subs, readiness was so important that we would drill for everything, from the everyday to unusual and potentially life-threatening dangers such as fire. Drilling is so important to readiness that I spend more time on the topic in chapter 7.

One readiness simulation I recall clearly illustrates the need for preparation. We were pulling into a port in the Caribbean to complete a simulated attack exercise on vessels in the harbor. This attack could occur by land, sea, or air. Our mission was to disable the ships in the harbor and show the weakness of their preparation. If we were not able to disable their ships, we knew they had prepared well. Importantly, when I served on submarines, we were always preoccupied with system failure. In fact, hospitals around the country have adopted a system called *high reliability*, which came from the navy and focuses on a preoccupation with preparing for system failure so that risk is mitigated.

In the Caribbean exercise, our mission was to send US Navy SEALS into the harbor where they were to attach simulated C-4 charges (actually, dye packs) to the propeller shafts of the ships. The preparation started two weeks out. We had a reconnaissance satellite and sent a reconnaissance team prior to the mission, which was scheduled for a very dark night with a new moon. We launched this mission on a SEAL delivery vehicle (SDV), which resides in a dry deck shelter on top of the sub's weapons shipping hatch. We approached the port two to three miles out and launched the SDV with SEALS and an explosive ordinance detail. Now keep in mind that many of these SEALs were hanging on to this device while wearing full gear, including tanks, masks, and flippers. The team went in under dark of night and attached the simulated C-4 explosives to the propeller shafts. The ships in the port had no idea this attack was happening. The C-4 was attached with timers so the dye packs would go off after the team cleared the area.

Our mission was successful. The ships' crews' preoccupation with failure did not work for the vessels in the port that day. If this had been a real sabotage, several ships would have been disabled for months by a handful of men. This type of preparation has also had a significant impact on police forces around the country. When it comes to system failure preparation, police forces are ready for domestic violence, robberies, and shoot-outs. But readiness in terms of the human element—deescalating a volatile situation, calming a distressed person, reacting to something that appears to be violent but really isn't, such as a child putting his hand in his pocket—could be drilled and tested in scenario after scenario, reducing the chance of an unnecessary shooting. And if zero tolerance for racial profiling were the norm and police officers, through training and drills, could quickly identify danger and respond with the appropriate force, then unintentional violence could be reduced. The well-known mantra of "protect and serve" appears on most police cars around the country. Training to protect is robust, but training and readiness to serve the public? Not so much.

Conflict Is Normal and Healthy

Conflict between police forces and communities today is not an example of positive conflict. By *conflict*, we're referring to a culture where issues are discussed openly and are not allowed to fester. This type of conflict can be necessary to accomplish the mission, especially when a lack of clarity could jeopardize the mission.

On a submarine, ignoring issues rarely happens, which in the long run reduces the number of bow diesel conflicts, those rare conversations that land both participants in the infirmary. The Society for Human Resource Managers (SHRM) reports that every unaddressed conflict wastes about eight hours of company time in gossip and unproductive activities. A good place to start addressing conflicts, according to SHRM, is realizing that conflict is normal and healthy. A culture where dissent is allowed and even encouraged can spur innovation and create diverse points of view. When I served on subs, diverse points of view were welcome if the mission was clear and fighting the submarine was a priority. Diverse points of view rarely caused problems. Problems were caused because someone wasn't contributing to the mission. Because so much was at risk when one person failed to fight the submarine, conflicts were not, generally, extended. If they were, they became time wasters. Even bow diesel conflicts were quickly over once they reached the point of physical violence. They were left in the bow diesel engine room and everyone went on to complete the mission.

A good place to start addressing conflicts, according to the SHRM, is realizing that conflict is normal and healthy.

In my years on submarines, I only knew of one bow diesel conflict, although there were rumors about them over the years. In this particular case, an issue came up between two men who disagreed on mostly everything, a situation that was exacerbated by the cramped space, foul air, and lack of privacy. Mediation was attempted in all the standard ways: swearing, stories, wit against wit, but to no avail. The two men met in the bow diesel engine room, turned off the sonar, and solved their issues the old-fashioned way: with fists flying. Later we saw them both in the wardroom, which doubled as an infirmary, getting their scratches, gouges, and bruises nursed. No one mentioned what had happened and no one asked for details. It wasn't necessary. There was peace between them after the bow diesel conflict.

In Deb's and my experience, accusatory statements, defensive or inflammatory language, and unwillingness to listen can provoke conflicts and fuel them. As a submariner, I learned that if an accusatory comment brought about a discussion revealing a problem with a sea daddy or sailor, or served as motivation to complete a task—for example, telling a new crewman he was slow in qualifying for watch because he was lazy—then it was more than an accusatory statement. It was direct, just not polite.

Deb's experience with conflict in the workplace was similar in that the unsaid can be far more destructive than the spoken. She is a direct communicator who expects others to lay their cards on the table as she does, and she has been known to address something as slight as rolled eyes during a presentation to get the real meaning of that body language out in the open. As a result, she builds teams quickly, and she roots out conflict before getting back to the mission at hand.

Many years ago, Deb successfully managed conflict as a change agent. The situation involved a talented disruptor who was focused on gossip and taking a negative attitude to every decision made in the organization. She was so negative that today we would call her *actively disengaged*, which refers to someone who is destructive to the organization. Deb brought her into her office, addressed the issue, as I had with the seaman apprentice from Philly (language cleaned up for business), and within three weeks put her in charge of a small team working on a specific initiative. The former disruptor had natural leadership ability and once she became engaged with the team and then the organization, she became a rock star performer. If left unaddressed, this issue would have created team problems and eventually organizational problems.

Whether in the military, in business, or in any organization, healthy conflict is essential to achieving the mission.

DEEP DIVE

WHAT IS YOUR ORGANIZATION'S MISSION?

What if goals in your organization or community were so clear that you had the freedom to operate but no time to waste? Would any organization knowingly spend time on petty stuff if the mission were crystal clear? A clear mission statement (one that is more about what the organization is today rather than a vision aimed at some point in the future) provides the framework for operating and achieving the mission on a day-to-day basis. Some companies hang their overall mission and vision statements on the wall without integrating them in the day-to-day mission. As a submariner, I found that mission was everything, even if it was just qualifying for watch instead of the more exciting mission of protecting the country from some threat or other in the Atlantic. Clear missions, clear norms, and a clear system overall consistently delivered the same result on submarines: inclusion.

If you don't have a clear mission statement as a guiding principle of your day-to-day mission, get one. It is critical to inclusion. Without clear boundaries and goals necessary for the mission to be accomplished, teams break down and the mission breaks down. From my experience and Deb's twenty-five-plus years in business, it is not possible to build strong, inclusive teams without a clear mission.

Three Questions about Your Organization's Mission

1. If asked, would your mid-level managers provide the same answer about your mission? Every submarine chief would.

2. Is your organization's mission reviewed and adjusted at least quarterly with significant input from mid-level managers?

3. Does the entire team understand how the mission contributes to their daily responsibility?

Feeling the vibe in Costa Rica.

Snow everywhere on John and Deb's wedding day.

Relaxing in the sun at home.

The vibe continues in Costa Rica.

Mom and Deb.

Acting silly on a night out.

Walking Mylee on a fall day in the Western N.C. foothills.

Mylee does love her walks, especially when it is cool outside . . .

John's son and daughter.

The log home, "Pura Vida" in Western N.C.

Somewhat relaxed uniform of the day during training onboard the Donald P. Hall.

Post-deployment / patrol awards ceremony.

CAPT Brad and John at his retirement.

John and Dad at his parents' home in Peterborough.

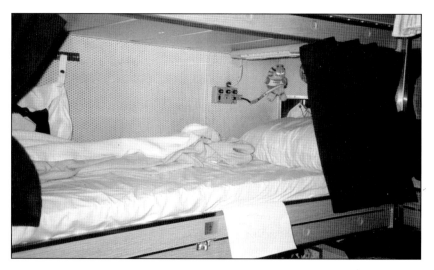

Plenty of room for two. This is a larger rack than what is found on fast attacks.

Wedding day at city hall in New York City.

John's Dad with him at senior enlisted academy graduation dinner.

"Deb made me inclue this . . . 'nuff said."

The snow just kept coming . . .

Wedding day at New York City Hall. Lots of snow, so we went with Plan B on wedding attire.

John's retirement ceremony. L: John's CO, CAPT Deets. R: : John's buddy and guest speaker CAPT Brad.

The Vincent family reunion prior to John's Dad's passing. John's Mom and Dad are in the front row.

Receiving company honor recruit award during basic training graduation ceremony.

PART II

THE ANCHORS OF
THE SYSTEM

ANCHORS OF THE SYSTEM

TRAINING

LEADERSHIP

MAKING GOOD DECISIONS

ROI OF THE SYSTEM

CHAPTER 7

DRILL, DRILL, DRILL: CULTURE TO FIGHT THE SUBMARINE

Aboard the submarine, we understood that we were hundreds of feet below the ocean and that a fire in the machinery space containing the oxygen generator could kill us. Yes, fire and oxygen are a lethal combination, but it was much worse. This is what happens in the oxygen generator: seawater is purified by separating the hydrogen and the oxygen. The oxygen is stored in case the oxygen generator goes down and the hydrogen is diffused, slowly bubbling out of the submarine. The problem is that oxygen is being made while there's hydrogen on board. Now that's a combination: fire, oxygen, and hydrogen. Does that sound like a bomb? We lived with the idea that, at any point, we could have a fire and if the fire wasn't put out immediately, we would have a very big, loud, and lethal problem.

So how did we live with the knowledge that each day could be "the day"? We drilled and drilled, scenario after scenario, so that responding to an emergency was second nature. We also qualified for watch to ensure every crew member on board knew how the submarine was supposed to operate so the crew would recognize when it wasn't operating properly.

How did drilling lead to better inclusion? We never forgot the mission. We drilled the current mission, we drilled survival, we drilled and drilled until we had a singular focus on mission and survival.

How did drilling lead to better inclusion? We never forgot the mission. We drilled the current mission, we drilled survival, we drilled and drilled until we had a singular focus on mission and survival. When you are that focused on the mission, petty day-to-day stuff just doesn't seem significant. About now you may be asking what that has to do with inclusion in your business. You might also think that fear of a significant emergency brings people together naturally, but that idea couldn't be further from the truth. The more stressful the situation, the more polarizing the culture can become.

HUMAN EXPERIENCE AND CULTURE CHANGE

Phil Geldart, the CEO of Eagle's Flight, an organization that uses experiential training to deliver cultural change, has a deep understanding of the human experiences that drive cultural transformations and takes a special interest in the correlations between experimental learning and cultural change.

When Deb interviewed Phil for this chapter, they talked about experiential learning in the navy, such as wearing a hood during drilling to simulate smoke because smoke from a fire limits visibility. She asked Phil if this kind of training was experiential, and he said, "Absolutely."

There's a natural parallel between the kind of experiential training the navy did and what Phil's company espouses. In the interview with Phil, Deb described what happened on the USS *Wyoming* and asked for Phil's thoughts on the topic. (We will discuss the USS *Wyoming* in chapter 9, but an overview of the challenge appears below). How could the US Navy successfully shift from an all-male submarine force to an integrated male and female submarine force and not just accommodate women but also make a cultural transformation that is fully inclusive of women? Phil said that the culture change would not be successful without respect, insight, and appreciation. Behavior is a byproduct of the existence of these three things, or the result if these are absent.

Phil's definition of respect is to appreciate the human being who is serving your food, an officer on your submarine, or your teacher in school. It is to understand all things, forgive all things, and appreciate another's point of view. It is to see people as human beings and not as a nationality or a group. When we talked to people about the things that make us human, such as our mother, father, or pet, we no longer see people as the wrappers we put around them, but instead, we see into the soul of the human being within. Esteem goes beyond rank or experience. Phil explained that Eagle's Flight does experiential training that includes how to be a human being and he gave an example: "We did some training in Mumbai a while back. Sue facilitated; a woman in a room full of Iranians, Iraqi's, and other nationalities—all male, I might add. In collaboration with this group, she presented 'Promises, Promises', an experiential learning program that reveals how we collaborate and interact in stressful situations and how to be more effective in those situations, is a very real way of showing the importance of collaboration while making clear the consequences of not collaborating." The concept of respect is way too important to address only in terms of a simple definition, or as an academic concept, or merely the right thing to do, which is how many diversity training programs approach it. As I have said throughout this book, appealing to our desire for knowledge or our desire to do what's right is not enough. Phil has it right. Learning to respect experientially is the key to understanding.

Learning to respect experientially is the key to understanding.

Phil Geldart defines insight as understanding the law of unexpected consequences. There is a way, in a simulated setting, to get people to experience what happens when they put their hand in a machine to fix it and they get injured, and then to understand the impact on the family when they're not working for eight weeks while they're healing. The guy's wife may have to go back to work, bills may pile up—the consequences can mount. Safety programs that get individuals to experience what happens when there's a safety violation have the most lasting impact. The result of this simulation has been a reduction in safety incidents wherever this kind of training takes place. Back on the sub, drilling, training, and learning were very hands on. One of the reasons why inclusion happened was because the consequences of not working together were so clear. If we didn't work together to put out a fire, we could die. What if your organization made the consequences of not working together very clear, and provided the hands-on, humanity-based experiential training necessary to achieve cultural change? If you still struggle with any kind of systemic diversity challenges, not limited to an individual, you have not changed your culture.

Appreciation should be the response to diversity, regardless of whether that diversity is created by ethnicity, gender, or a diverse point of view. People who are different from you can add a lot to your life when you spend time with them. When social groups work together, they generate appreciation as well as improved productivity and efficiency. Phil observes that when you spend time with people who are different from you, you see beyond the color of their skin to what they're really about.

Phil's innate and proven knowledge of experiential learning has convinced him that someone who appears to be prejudiced (and in my view, that's all of us) should be asked to spend time with those they are prejudiced against. Take urban youth and police officers playing basketball with each other, for example. When police only receive training for risk prevention, they have the equivalent of the proverbial hammer: "if all you have is a hammer, then everything is a nail." But if you encourage this kind of experiential training off the job, when risk is minimal, and not on the job, when risk is high, you can proactively build better relationships. The humanity of urban youth and the humanity of police officers create an imprint that changes behavior forever.

ACHIEVING CULTURAL TRANSFORMATION: DRILL INTO CULTURE MORE THAN LEADERSHIP

This chapter talks about creating real, lasting change that results in inclusion. One of these ways is through drilling, or experiential learning. But in the case of your organization or community, what change would you be preparing for? Most organizations are so far from fostering inclusion that the change they seek is not easy to see. What they seek is a total transformation of the culture. Phil Geldart says a true cultural transformation should outlast the management that initiated it. We agree. On submarines, it doesn't matter what kind of sub you're on or how young or new the crew is because The System keeps inclusion in place. The culture is sustained even though the leadership and crew change frequently. Many large organizations seeking cultural change resort to changing senior leadership, some going as far as to offer expensive packages to change their culture.

One organization Deb worked for replaced 70 percent of their experienced managers. This kind of drastic approach risks client relationships, costs a good deal of money (at least initially), and changes the culture only slowly because experienced managers are replaced with inexperienced employees. Changing cultures to improve inclusion can be achieved with the existing team. The key is to employ the right system. The Submarine Way employs proven leadership and experiential training, eliminating only those stuck in the old, biased system.

So, how can your organization execute The System, drill or train through experiential training, and change the culture to a truly inclusive culture? In my experience, it is through peer pressure from those who have a commitment to inclusion that I would call tribal. And this tribal commitment is passed to new generations through role modeling. This is a significant piece of experiential learning. If commitment to inclusion isn't role-modeled by the leaders, it doesn't stick. How critical leadership is to inclusion will be discussed in the next chapter. The important fact to remember here is that, on submarines, commitment is merely lip service from a new crew member, but three years later, that crew member wants to pass on this tribal survival skill to the new crew because it works. The culture sticks and lives beyond the current management, just as Phil claims.

Deb's experience with cultural transformations also parallels my own. She recalls that when leaders in the organizations she has worked with embraced cultural change, she knew that change had a real shot at sticking. Her hallmark of a successful transformation was that when she checked back with an organization she had previously assisted, she found the culture she had brought to that organization had stuck. When she improved the client feedback survey at one company she worked with, the new culture never deteriorated. There were new processes, training structures, and role modeling of the new expectations.

We use the words *commitment* and *embrace* to talk about what's needed to make a true cultural change. Phil calls this conviction. Phil's definition of conviction is that hearts and minds are engaged in the process of change. Our experience is that this does not happen overnight. The System needs to be in place, people need to be trained experientially in it, and it needs to be role-modeled so that it creates a permanent imprint on the culture. The powerful way we did this on submarines was to drill for the success of the endeavor, or mission. The crew's sense of mission success built commitment and drove us toward a successful culture.

However, even with the most effective experiential learning and even with mission success, individual crew members did not always see eye to eye. Persistent conflicts of this kind and bow diesel conflicts in particular have been a topic of conversation between Deb and me, and we have discussed how they relate to conflict in a business setting. In fact, internal conflicts can often act as the best opportunity to drill certain cultural values into your company. We agree that direct but not personal conflict can lead to better outcomes. Crucial conversations ensure that nothing festers. The unwritten rule is that you don't go to your boss with an issue; you solve it quickly and probably at high volume, and then you move on. Deb wishes businesses were more open to direct communication within their organizations so issues don't fester. Her personal brand has been to get the conflict out in the open and facilitate discussion to solve the issue. Being polite about the problem is good, but if politeness doesn't sufficiently expose the issue, then the next step might be to have each person talk about the grievance, unreservedly, without filters, and in detail.

The areas of overlap between Deb's direct conflict resolution and The Submarine Way are significant. The point here is to build direct and open communication, solve the issue at the lowest common denominator, and empower the parties involved to move past the issue quickly. It is important to integrate and embrace this model for conflict resolution as soon as conflicts arise. The common misunderstanding that "time heals all wounds," that a problem will just "blow over," guarantees an issue will fester and run counter to an inclusive culture. One of the best signs of an inclusive environment is when we can admit we have a problem and there's openness and a commitment to work it out.

Earlier we discussed various ways to avoid unhealthy conflict and create a climate conducive to deepening a state of inclusion, which, however, doesn't mean an environment is conflict-free. Tension caused by marital problems, health or child issues, or even bad traffic can cause a build-up of stress. These events have a genetically programmed fight-or-flight effect on our body. In most cases, once that fight-or-flight effect is activated, stress sits in our body until it's released. If it isn't, it can lead to disease.

Of course, I'm certainly not saying that fighting is the right solution to dealing with stress, and despite the closeness, tension, and boredom on a submarine, this kind of bow diesel conflict resolution was rare during my navy service. What I am saying, however, is that dealing with conflict directly and openly is good on many levels. Don't let your work environment be damaged by a culture that refuses to drill in a conflict resolution model. Conflict can be caused by the actual or perceived difference in values and interests between people who work together, or within an organizational structure. (We discussed conflict in great detail in chapter 6 for those wanting a refresher.)

DEEP DIVE

DOES YOUR ORGANIZATION NEED A CULTURAL RENOVATION?

Do you have the conviction to improve your organization's culture and get it to stick? Below are six questions to help you understand your culture better. If two or more of these show you have an inclusion, culture, or leadership issue, all three likely need attention:

1. Does your organization have a culture of inclusion?

2. Is your culture in need of a transformation?

3. Do you have advocates who can role-model and lead the initiative?

4. Do you know what this effort's outcome will be? Can you describe it?

5. Do you have leaders who can hold others accountable for this vision?

6. Do you have experiential training or drilling resources to reinforce this change?

CHAPTER 8

CAPTAIN OF THE SHIP: LEADERSHIP AND ITS IMPORTANCE TO INCLUSION

Deb recalls a situation that occurred to her many years ago at a time when women, especially women responsible for an all-male sales team, were not easily accepted (to say the least). Deb was known for her focus on mission, her professionalism, and her no-nonsense attitude. When her boss called her in one day to tell her she needed to be "nicer" to the outside sales team, she asked what that meant. Her boss told her she was an attractive woman and would be a lot more popular with the sales team if she had dinner or drinks with them on a social basis. Yes, the leader of this organization set a dangerous precedent and, in fact, was ensuring true inclusion would not happen there. He may or may not have been surprised at her reaction. She quietly got up and walked out of his office. She did not have drinks or go out to dinner with the sales team, just to be more popular. She loved the company, but she left it a few years later because the culture did not support or respect women. Her team was very successful there, sales were up, and customer satisfaction was off the charts. The leadership was bewildered that she would leave such a promising career.

Good leadership is critical to a truly inclusive environment.

Good leadership is critical to a truly inclusive environment. Good leaders ensure that The System is in place, build other leaders to ensure that The System stays in place, and also build commitment or, as Phil Geldart calls it, conviction. Leaders who institutionalize bias, stereotyping, or harassment undermine the very fabric of the organization and the culture. A culture supporting any of these elements cannot be sustained for long.

MEETING THE CAPTAIN

Captain McDonald was the most unusual leader I've ever worked for, and the story of when I met him says a lot about both of us. I was a bit of a pirate in the early days of my career, engaging in the usual navy stuff, such as swearing, and drinking, and swashbuckling. The day Captain Bradley McDonald and I met for the first time was on the pier. I was aware a new commanding officer was coming onboard that day and I can't recall why I wasn't more prepared, but there I stood, no cover, dirty poopy suit, smoking a cigarette, and wearing quite a bit of stubble from several days of avoiding a razor. He saluted me, looking perfect in his uniform, a third generation Annapolis graduate and commanding officer of a submarine. Then there was me, excellent at what I did as an assistant navigator but pretty much an unconventional navy chief. I was the youngest chief and no one worked harder, slept less, and got more done than I did. I was obsessive back then and, truth be told, I still am a bit. He didn't blink at the way I looked, or dress me down, which I deserved. Two things struck me about him that day: his poise and the fact he was clearly in control and chose not to address my appearance. He immediately had my respect, which wasn't—and still isn't—easy to gain.

My second meeting with him, for our first briefing, solidified my lifelong respect. He wanted to meet with me right away, and of course, I complied. Now we had just put in to port after being at sea for a very long time. After seeing me glance at my wristwatch several times, he asked, "Am I keeping you from something important, Chief?" I said, "Sir, I was hoping to be able to enjoy some port duty." Even though this was a critical first briefing, he said, "Sure, Chief, go ahead. I would not dream of interfering with your social time."

Let's just say this was a surprising response. There was one-part compassion in Captain McDonald that day and one-part "Are you kidding me? You just said that to the commanding officer of this boat?" Those two reactions won me over. I am a lifelong fan of his leadership and he has plenty of other fans as well. I attended another retirement celebration a few years back for a fellow enlisted crew member and had the pleasure of seeing Captain McDonald—now "Brad" since we'd both retired and become friends—along with a whole lot of other crew we'd served with. The years suddenly vanished and there we were, in our world, which we had never really left because it was so engrained. We were natural leaders, bolstered by experiential training, completely inclusive of all contributions, strengthened through The System, and totally supportive of each other. Captain McDonald was holding court, telling jokes, and showing us again that leaders are always leaders. He is my friend, always my leader, and a role model throughout my life.

Ultimately, without leadership, The System doesn't happen. It is not sustained from crew to crew, and you don't build new leaders. Of

> **Ultimately, without leadership, The System doesn't happen. It is not sustained from crew to crew, and you don't build new leaders**

course, inclusion is not the only thing that leaders are responsible for, but what happens when many, or even a few, do not feel included? There is a breakdown in the team that becomes irrevocable, so correct it early and build inclusion through a system. In my days of naval service I found that submarine chiefs took their duty very seriously, so seriously that we had a "Chief's Creed." (Please keep in mind that chiefs are mid-level supervisors who have the most influence over the rank and file.).

What would it do for businesses or for communities if every mid-level manager took their responsibility so seriously that they had a creed? Here are a few of the important words of the "Chief's Creed":

> *By performance and testing you have been advanced on this day to Chief Petty Officer. The rank of E7 only in the United States Navy, carries with it unique responsibilities and privileges you are now bound to observe and expected to fulfill. Your entire way of life is now changed. You have not just been promoted one paygrade but promoted into an elite fellowship and as in most fellowships you have a special responsibility to your comrades, even as they have special responsibility to you. Your new responsibilities do not appear in print.*

They have no official standing. They cannot be referred to by name, number or file. They have existed for over 100 years. Their actions and their performance demand the respect of their seniors and their juniors. It is now required of you to be the fountain of wisdom, the ambassador of good will, the authority in personal relations as well as in technical applications. You have made the term," ask the chief", a household name in and out of the Navy.

There's a lot more to the "Chief's Creed," but you get the idea. These are larger-than-life leaders, who are selfless and have emotional intelligence, even if they express themselves at full volume with colorful language. They have a duty to be inclusive, get the best from everyone, and be the fountain of wisdom for anyone who needs it.

TACTICAL READINESS: DEVELOPING LEADERS

Every organization and community needs a fountain of wisdom, someone who puts comrades first, develops people, promotes based on results, and is colorblind. I would suggest that, in this age of selfish leaders who are more focused on their ambition, selfless and wise leaders are in even greater demand.

Developing and training leaders would fill a whole book, but identifying natural leaders, as opposed to selecting leaders only from people with expertise in a specific area, requires identifying certain characteristics:

1. A natural leader is the heart and the head of whom and what they are leading. Captain McDonald had a great heart

and a great head. He instinctively knew how to get the best from me. Promoting a leader who is all head and no heart will always be a struggle. You might get temporary results, but the big picture will be compromised.

2. A natural leader often doesn't set out to lead. Deb said she started managing large numbers of people at the age of twenty-three because she rose to the top of potential leaders, all considerably younger than she was. In her early twenties, she was responsible for getting above-average commitment from her team and better than average results. Her natural tendency is to lead, even without a leadership title.

3. A natural leader influences and directs results. If the leader you are considering for your team does not have *influence* over others but only *power*, choose someone else.

4. A natural leader is independent but inclusive. When I talked to Captain McDonald about this chapter and told him we would focus on leadership and its influence on inclusion, he said, "I never thought about inclusion, but nothing less than full inclusion was ever acceptable to me. I was focused on leading and building leaders. What they looked like, talked like, or where they came from was not important. It was leadership I was looking for."

5. A natural leader communicates. We've talked about verbal and nonverbal communication in previous chapters and the ability to see and diffuse conflict. Natural leaders don't get others spun up in their language; they get everyone focused on the mission through their ability to communicate the mission clearly and with passion.

Part of building crew-munity to have successful missions was dealing with those who did not buy into the mission and were disruptive. Business would call this a change management issue. It can also be an employee issue, meaning you've selected and hired the wrong person. Whatever the reason or result, it has to be dealt with or the mission is in jeopardy. How this is successfully dealt with challenges all leaders.

These issues also occur in the business world; individuals can create great disruption in the operation of the business if they're not checked. When I served on submarines, issues were dealt with at the lowest possible level. There were times when pressures did build up and conflicts couldn't be resolved by talking them out, which often led to the bow diesel engine room solution. Resolution of some types of conflict often require that leaders understand this is not their fight. Today I would say that leaders needed to be discerning, and by allowing solutions to be worked out by the crew, they allow crew-munity to occur. This, however, is truly a leadership decision. Without that discernment, leaders would become too involved in day-to-day opera-tions. Just as Captain McDonald decided

> **The most exceptional leadership is the kind that is discerning.**

not to address the issue of my conduct his first day on the boat, the most exceptional leadership is the kind that is discerning.

As I mentioned earlier, even when your team has great focus on the mission and bias is replaced with inclusion, there are times when two people just can't get along, such as in a bow diesel conflict. What do you do when this happens in your organization? Are leaders there to promote dealing with the issue, using discernment to achieve the right solution? Or do they allow these issues to go unaddressed?

YOUR LEADERSHIP PRINCIPLES

BY CAPTAIN BRADLEY MCDONALD

Do you have leadership principles? Have you defined yourself as a leader? Most of us who are interested in the concept of leadership are willing to read books written by noteworthy leaders, attend leadership classes and seminars, and engage in leadership retreats and activities. However, most of us have never actually written down our own leadership principles or philosophy, or attempted to define ourselves as leaders. Coming up in the US Navy, I observed that my COs had their own command policy letter, which was part of one's check-in/welcome-aboard package upon reporting to the ship. By chance, I came upon the idea of making that letter my leadership philosophy and added to it my leadership principles. Creating your own leadership principles will help you define yourself as a leader.

> **Most of us have never actually written down our own leadership principles or philosophy, or attempted to define ourselves as leaders.**

In the year prior to taking command, an event that most seagoing officers will testify to as the pinnacle of their career, I thought back over the seven COs I had on four previous ships. I wrote down their admirable and effective leadership traits, as well as those that were less than admirable and, occasionally, downright harmful to running an efficient ship. Also, taking advantage of the large pool of post command officers who wanted little more than to relive their glory days, I sought out many to interview at the Pentagon, where I was stationed. Simply, I asked them, "In retrospect, what worked well for you in command and what did not?" From those experiences I wrote a list of what I called CO guidelines. I carried this list in my pocket notepad and looked at it daily during my three years in command. There is nothing remarkable about the list; it is just seven simple tips to which I held myself accountable and still do when I'm in a leadership position. Here's the original list:

1. Be approachable and in control of yourself. If you can't control yourself, the crew won't believe you can control the ship.

2. Be yourself but always be the CO.

3. Be consistent.

4. Be fair and just.

5. Set standards and stick to them. The CO decrees the standards.

6. Continuously supply energy and enthusiasm for what is to be done.

7. Make the troops proud that you are their CO!

Now I'll expand a bit on each of these.

Be approachable and in control of yourself. A leader's first task in life is to have self-control. Have you had a boss who came unglued, maybe apoplectic, at the hint of bad news? Then he takes it out on those around him? If a leader does not possess self-control and act out calmness of mind in the tough situations that come his way, people are going to become reluctant to bring him bad news. Once your people stop bringing you the bad news, you're really in trouble.

In 1989 a US Navy submarine collided with a large navy supply ship while attempting to pass it in the outbound channel from Norfolk, Virginia. As the submarine maneuvered to pass, the focus of the bridge and periscope personnel (at least six sets of eyes total) became a buoy (on the left side of the channel) into which the sub was being sent by the current. The CO kept ordering his ship to the right, apparently not realizing that he was steering right into the large ship he was attempting to pass. Too late, he looked to the right, realized collision was imminent, and ordered emergency maneuvers, which served to mitigate the damage, but not avoid the impact.

One might wonder how, with all those trained sets of eyes, not one person yelled, "Captain, we're about to drive into the supply ship!" Actually, I think it is quite plausible, because I knew that CO. He was a man who rarely, if ever, controlled his outbursts. His primary form of leading was yelling and scowling, publicly and privately. He never welcomed bad news or his subordinates' recommendations. As he shut down all meaningful input from his crew, they realized he did not welcome or even want their feedback. He did things his way, and that was it. To make a suggestion was to get yelled at, rebuked, or humiliated. So, as bizarre as it seems, I can imagine that at least one lookout, if not more, realized the situation was becoming dire but, having been conditioned to the dangers of making recommendations to this captain, said nothing. Simply put, this CO was not approachable and, generally, seen as not in control of himself.

Here's a helpful rule of thumb you can live by and promise to your team.

Any time you bring me bad news, I will listen calmly. (Of course, if the situation requires immediate action, I expect you to take that action first.) I will ask you questions and the more information you can give me, the better. If, on the other hand, you choose to keep bad news from me, and I find that out through other channels, then stand by, as you will likely become a target for me, and I won't be so calm.

In summary, I believe that nothing builds the crew's faith in their captain as much as two things do: his calm, decisive, and intelligent response to emergency and peril at sea, and his willingness to listen to ideas and feedback from his crew.

Be yourself but always be the Commanding Officer. After having had seven COs, and sometimes standing in awe of a few of them, I could easily have thought I needed to be just like them, that I did not have innate CO quality material of my own. I had to tell myself I already possessed what it took to do that job; I didn't have to try to be somebody else. I needed to be me—while avoiding being "one of the guys." To keep that from being a problem, I reminded myself daily that the men needed me to be their *captain*, not their pal, their drinking buddy, or their BFF. They needed a leader they could look up to and follow. I should not forget that I was a commanding officer but humbly and politely embrace that role and *never* shy away from it.

Be consistent. People would rather work for a jerk every day than a jerk one day, Mr. Nice Guy the next day, and an unknown quantity the third day. Don't keep the crew guessing on what you expect or how you're going to act. If you act consistently, they will respond consistently. No guessing games.

Be fair and just. Oh no, it's the dreaded *F* word. We tell our children that life is not fair (and fair is so subjective, so why even attempt it?). As a commanding officer, I had a lot of power over 125 lives. I could control their liberty, cut their pay, and reduce them in rank, along with a host of other painful restrictions I could easily impose. It was important to me that I could look myself in the mirror at the end of each day and say, "Today I did all I could to demonstrate fairness and justice in my actions with my men."

Set standards and stick to them. The CO sets the standards. The key point here is that leaders set standards by their actions or by their inactions. Either way, the leader sets the standards. When I was eleven years old, my father was the executive officer (number two to the CO) on a large ship with a crew of over 1,200. One Saturday I was on the ship with him, and as we were leaving, walking along the long main deck, he stopped, told me to wait, and walked off. When he returned, he had a roving watch stander in tow. He pointed to a small oil leak under a drain pipe and told the watch to get it cleaned up. Then he and I continued our walk to the bow. Later I asked him why he had to deal with such small things as a little oil leak. He said, "Once I walk over oil on the deck, a clear message has been sent to the other 1,198 men that oil on the deck is okay. We'll have oil everywhere."

In general, it's not realistic to expect that people will set a standard in any area that is higher than that which they see from their leader. Don't expect your people to maintain a better personal appearance than you. Don't expect them to use better language than you. Don't expect them to be more positive than you. Don't expect them to follow rules you don't follow. Don't expect them to pick up a piece of trash on the floor if they saw you walk over it. In short, don't expect people ranked below you to ever reach for a higher standard than what they see from you. You are always setting the standards!

Continuously supply energy and enthusiasm for what is to be done. This is similar to the previous tip about setting standards. Every job has its grunt work and most of us don't like doing it. A leader needs to set the standard for putting energy and enthusiasm into the grunt work. On a submarine, frequently a mishmash of overworked and sleep-deprived sailors, there is plenty of grunt work. During my years of service, the least popular of all was field day, a three to four-hour period of all hands cleaning the ship. I told the leaders and myself that we *all* cleaned during field day, happily, energetically, and enthusiastically. Don't expect your crew to put more energy into the task at hand than they see coming from you.

Make the troops proud that you are their CO! There is no formula for this, but I knew I wanted my men to think, *I'm glad that guy is my captain. I'll gladly follow him anywhere.* With that in mind, I realized that if I took care of my men, they would take care of the ship and they would have what they wanted: a man they were proud to call their captain.

Take some time and make a stab at creating your own leadership principles. They do not have to be complex. Simple is better. Once you have created those principles—perhaps they are principles that already guide your life and leadership—look at them every day. Make sure you define yourself as the leader you want to be.

DEEP DIVE

IS YOUR LEADERSHIP SUPPORTIVE OF INCLUSION, AS WELL AS THE BUILDING OF FUTURE LEADERSHIP TALENT?

Here are five questions for your organization to ask to evaluate your leadership:

1. Are your middle managers prepared to pass on leadership traditions and hold up the values of the organization?

2. Do your managers know your company mission?

3. What kind of training and support do your managers receive?

4. Are your middle managers selected because they have subject matter expertise or because they show leadership ability?

5. Do you have a leadership mentor program?

6. Do your leaders use influence or power to accomplish the mission?

CHAPTER 9

DON'T GET BILGED ON YOUR OWN ANCHOR: MISTAKES, SELF-REGULATION, AND NORMS

The title of this chapter is an old nautical term referring to literally piercing the ship's hull with its own anchor. Needless to say, not a good thing, not a good day.

We talked about the importance of norms and self-regulation in other chapters, alluding to pressure and even forms of punishment to correct unacceptable behavior. We also talked about the fact that it was rarely an option to get a chief or other leader involved with day-to-day conflicts. Think about the blanket party in chapter 3 and the rank of that group inflicting bruises and black eyes to manage unacceptable behavior. Since I was one of them, I can say that this situation was not going to be raised to a chief or petty officer to resolve unless we couldn't resolve it. While these are surely extreme examples and not what we would want to package for society at large, the self-regulation and self-discipline of the submarine navy can teach us a lot about expectations and norms. Does it always work? Well, no.

The submarine navy has received some negative publicity regarding diversity. It doesn't like a lot of publicity, negative or otherwise. Why do you think they call it the silent service? Recent negative publicity stemmed from one particular news story: In 2014, several women officers on the USS *Wyoming* were video-taped showering or changing clothes. One low-ranking individual shot the videotapes, and other sailors of similar rank viewed them. Until that moment, the submarine force had perceived itself as successfully integrating women into the submarine crew, using The System that I am familiar with. Women have, for the most part, felt included and in the several years since the beginning of integration there has been silence, all preferred by the submarine force. But then there was this failure of The System, of norms, and of self-discipline. What happened? Does this mean that regulations from the top, as well as punishment, must come from a guiding force?

If an anchor is good because it holds you in place in the water, what must it be if you run over your own anchor? A bit of a mess, right?

When I decided the title for this chapter, it seemed fitting, considering the topic. If an anchor is good because it holds you in place in the water, what must it be if you run over your own anchor? A bit of a mess, right? So, when social norms, rules, regulations, and even punishment fail in an organization that handles many of its conflicts internally, what then? It was determined after the trial that ten seamen—of close to 140 onboard—were involved in the distribution and viewing of the video. Leaders on other ships were the ones who blew the cover on the situation after gossip began to spread. Why did the leadership of the *Wyoming* not hear about the situation before others did and do something about it? It came out at the trial that the videotaping had been going on for ten months.

The anchor in this case was the crew. The crew runs the ship along with the leadership. There are fourteen or fifteen officers on a modern submarine, but by and large it's the crew that handles internal conflict, establishes norms, and makes sure the inclusion system is in place and operating (either consciously or unconsciously). They apply pressure to the new seamen to qualify for watch, or gain any other qualification that is needed, because fighting a submarine means the training never stops. According to Navy Vice Admiral M. J. Connor, in a letter obtained by CNN, "Incidents that violate the trust of our sailors go against the core values of what we hold sacred. We go to war together with the confidence that we can rely on each other in all circumstances and this is a breach of trust."

The navy was humiliated and embarrassed. Its four-year effort at integration was deemed successful prior to this incident, and the *Wyoming* was the first submarine to integrate women officers. They had plans to integrate, first, female officers in fast attacks, and then enlisted female crew. They had to ask themselves whether their efforts had really been as successful as they had originally thought.

Comments from women who were part of the submarine force were revealing. In a *USA Today* article, dated December 9, 2015, Lieutenant Jennifer Carroll, who served on board the *Maine*, reported, "It was a shocking event. It was completely 180 degrees from what my experience was. I couldn't even fathom that one of our guys could do that to me." Carroll also went on to say that she felt like a sister to her shipmates on the *Maine*.

Other comments from Lieutenant Carroll fit my view of submarine life as well. She believed the submarine community is special because members of the crew become as close as family. In Lieutenant Carroll's experience, relationships with the crew were based on mutual respect and the *Wyoming* incident contradicted a universal sense of camaraderie among submariners. So how is an incident like that reconciled with the universal view that life on a submarine is one of mutual respect and healthy interdependence?

When investigators were through with their research, they pointed to one reason why the situation had lasted so long: peer pressure. They determined that nearly a dozen men knew about the spying but failed to report it for fear of breaching ties to their shipmates.

When investigators were through with their research, they pointed to one reason why the situation had lasted so long: peer pressure. They determined that nearly a dozen men knew about the spying but failed to report it for fear of breaching ties to their shipmates. This is clearly the other side of the coin to a life that is full of self-regulation and discipline. Loyalty held this dysfunction in place. Loyalty trumped trust as well. Does this event mar most submarine experiences, or devalue the inclusion system? In my opinion, no. It is simply proof that no system and no human is flawless.

SELF-REGULATION

When it comes to self-regulation, as human beings, we have a very basic need to belong, which drives behavior to ensure we will belong. Being a good group member requires the ability to self-regulate according to the norms of the group. We have talked positively in previous chapters about how norms can be so strong that they prohibit bias, keep crews focused on building relationships, and create trust that ensures the success of the mission. What happened on the *Wyoming* was the antithesis of all that we held important on submarines. The behavior of those ten men defied norms, broke trust, and was a contradiction of the need to belong and self-regulate to gain acceptance. Being a good group member requires decisions, some conscious and some not, that involve deciding what is best for the group and what is best for the individual. A good group member puts the group first. When one crew member puts his or her own interests above those of the group, whether it is stealing or spying, as on the *Wyoming*, inhibition breaks down. Knowing what to avoid, or when to stop is a core feature of self-regulation.

When researching the situation on the *Wyoming*, I came across an article about two submarine leaders who were fantasizing about one of the women who had been videotaped. During that discussion, one indicated he had a videotape of the woman and asked the other if he wanted to see it. Although the other submariner seemed to have no issue with the fantasy discussion, he was opposed to the act of taping and spying, so it was he who broke open the whole situation.

Although it is clearly more of an intrusion on privacy to tape and spy on another member of the crew, the first breakdown of trust occurs when action to inhibit impulse fails. To talk about a member of the crew in a lustful, sexual way invites actions to further the discussion and create a new norm. The crew of the *Wyoming*, or any military unit, should not have encouraged talk to become action. Such self-regulation is at the core of crew-munity. I could not imagine engaging in this kind of discussion among crew members, let alone taking it a step further as the young man did. Crew-munity is, as Lieutenant Carroll said, trust almost to the level of family. Not many would breach this kind of a trust in a family, and crew-munity is no different.

Multiple online posts that I came across while researching the *Wyoming* situation took the position that putting together men and women in their twenties made the videotaping incident inevitable. Some of these bloggers were young submariners and others had served with crews before the navy allowed female submarine crew and couldn't imagine serving with a female. Fortunately, however, this attitude was rare. Most of the opinions expressed were strongly negative toward objectifying crew and especially officers. Most bloggers took the attitude that women submariners are here, they are serving successfully, and are important, contributing crew members who should be accepted and normalized.

One blogger, who seemed to almost have inside information, suspected that the young petty officer who had started the videoing had an issue with women serving on submarines and holding leadership positions. Objectifying the officers was his way of taking away their authority and projecting his anger.

Whatever the videotaper's motives were, I believe the 24/7 nature of submarine existence intensifies the potential for lapses in The System, which makes it different from a business where someone objects to having to report to a male, a gay person, or a woman.

I bring the *Wyoming* incident up because I don't want to pretend that The System creates a perfect world and that there aren't lapses. The lesson learned from the *Wyoming* incident is to watch for lapses early and deal with them swiftly and with maximum severity. The young crewmember I spoke of earlier, who stole and was subjected to a blanket party, not only received punishment from his peers, but because the inspection was formal, he "went to mast" and was kicked out of the navy. Not one officer during the mast asked why he had bruises and a black eye. They didn't need to; they knew. Vigilantism is not a solution, but clear, swift accountability is.[3]

CONFORMING TO SOCIAL NORMS

There is considerable pressure to conform to social norms and the submarine is a microcosm, on steroids, of society's norms. Because the mission is ever changing, these norms sometimes change. However, if the command is consistent, the norms should never change. One of the strongest of the norms used to modify behavior is shunning. A definition of *shunning* is "to persistently ignore, avoid, or reject someone." No, this is not the kind of shunning described in Nathaniel Hawthorne's novel *The Scarlett Letter,* or anything that extreme. Shunning is used to motivate someone who is moving through the qualifying process too slowly, such as the shunning employed by the senior chief who wouldn't acknowledge the existence of new crew members until they qualified for watch. It's a very powerful motivator.

Acceptance is built into all of us social creatures. Rejection hits us hard. Consider the young man from Philadelphia who couldn't get along with anyone. He was practically shunned by everyone until he was told, directly, how to be accepted. He chose acceptance and success.

---

3   Now, I ignore comments made by a young lady or man about the sexuality of the bartender at the last port. These sailors are twenty-somethings, and it is not my job to regulate what they think or say about a port call. I pick my battles. My job is to teach crew members to be considerate of others who might be sensitive to explicit talk. This is the personal space sensitivity we talked about in chapter 3.

A solution to the problem of the videotaping of the *Wyoming's* female officers could have been shunning. I will always wonder why so many went along with something that did not fit the core values. Here's how that scenario would have played out from my experience: one by one, ten individuals would be socially avoided: no one would talk to them in the mess deck, and crew would only say what was necessary to them when relieving them from watch. Soon this would come to a chief's attention, and he would ask what the hell was going on. If the chief were doing his job, it would be days, not months, until the truth came to light.

WHEN SOCIAL NORMS BREAK DOWN

Norms are a healthy and robust way to drive certain core beliefs on a submarine, such as qualifying for watch, or encouraging trust and inclusion. When I discussed the importance of norms with Deb, she said she felt that anomie, the degradation of societal standards, is happening in society today. Her study of social science in college and grad school made clear the effect of anomie in society. Any rapid changes in society can result in anomie. The change that came about when women started joining the submarine force affected a few crewmen. On the *Wyoming*, some were so uprooted by the change that they could no longer abide by the strong norms in place and participated in unacceptable behavior. Others were so shaken by the change that they couldn't stop the unacceptable behavior. The most effective way for the navy to handle such anomie is to overly communicate norms and hold the crew responsible for maintaining them.

In 1973, Stanford University conducted a prison experiment to test the effects of dehumanizing prisoners. A group of individuals were arrested, given numbers, and had their identities taken away, thus starting the process of dehumanization. As time went on, the other study participants (who became the guards) started to treat the prisoners increasingly badly. The more the prisoners were dehumanized, the worse the treatment became. (Think Abu Ghraib in Iraq where, once the prisoners started to be dehumanized, their treatment escalated to sexual abuse, torture, rape, and murder.) The Stanford experiment was thought to have been sanctioned at the highest levels, but if the torture was carried out with some goal in mind, it soon sank to the level of becoming the objective, not the means of gaining of information. The point here is that when you reduce the status of an individual to less than who that person is—for example, turning an officer into a woman taking a shower—it becomes easier to escalate abhorrent behavior.

SIGNS OF A BREAKDOWN OF NORMS

Dehumanizing behavior: This includes using *antisocial* language to talk about other people behind their back. Antisocial language is language that doesn't stick to facts. Random gossip and backbiting breaks down the social network and needs to be addressed.

Shunning: Shunning that occurs because a crew member isn't qualifying for watch is different from shunning without a clear purpose. If, as a supervisor, you notice members of your team are avoiding one or more individuals, but there's little to no buzz, you should realize something is happening that you should not ignore. It could be bullying or an office affair between a manager and an employee.

You should make it your business to find out what the issue is and address it.

Unaddressed staff issues: Some leaders may be hesitant to address issues among their people because they fear reprisal. Their lack of action leads to low accountability, goals that are not consistently met, and negatively affected engagement.

Lack of respect for leaders: A situation in which a leader, or leaders, is not respected and there are clear undercurrents of undermining must be addressed before it incurs a negative outcome, including high turnover, unmet goals—or worse, your organization gains the attention of the news media.

These four signs of a breakdown in norms are common to all business settings and can often be avoided through transparency. For example, at Media General, I worked with two very strong-willed women, one responsible for sales and the other for traffic, or media scheduling. There was plenty of overlap of responsibility and conflicts did occur, such as when the salesperson promised the client a specific time for a commercial that the traffic manager couldn't accommodate. Think there was an opportunity for conflict there? These two women would really go at it. Each laid open all the issues of her role to the other, usually at top volume. But not once in the time I worked with them did their conflict ever get personal. When the salesperson went too far with pushing her agenda, often there were chocolates or donuts on Monday for the traffic manager. I am still friends with both and they are the best of friends today as they were back then.

Their system worked well for them because there was transparency. I watched for signs of a breakdown in norms when I first started to work with them, but what I learned was that their total transparency with each other, and us, built trust rather than broke it down.

STICK WITH THE SYSTEM

I am not going to second-guess the navy on how women were added to the submarine force: what was said, how it was announced, or what training was provided. Quite frankly, I don't know how the process was managed. But I will say that we were always successful with inclusion because of The System, the stages of inclusion we discussed in previous chapters, and direct communication, and also because, through trust, we were transparent with each other. In the case of the soap stealer, we suspected him for a number of reasons, but because he had never had the closeness, directness, or honesty of others, he was not viewed as transparent. I often suspect that we have gotten too careful with each other when we address concerns and we've lost transparency in the process. I believe healthy norms and self-regulation were maintained on the subs I served on because we were very transparent about our challenges, and we stayed focused on our mission. This was also true when I worked in the corporate world, at Media General.

Deb's experiences of transparency are both positive and negative. Those who don't want to face issues head on will not appreciate transparency. They will deny the potential challenges and not face obvious signs of trouble. They will not engage in a healthy above-board discussion as the salesperson and traffic manager did at Media General.

Why wasn't transparency being applied on the *Wyoming*? How could anyone on that boat have been focused on the mission? Why wasn't the issue being discussed loudly, in the way I remember communication onboard was conducted? How could the navy have created transparency in that situation?

The US Navy recently introduced a new ethics program that focused specifically on the *Wyoming* incident with a film clip of sailors sharing a cell phone video of a fellow female sailor showering. The navy claimed that the program was not based on real events. While ethics programs need to tell us what is and isn't appropriate behavior, my guess is that the sailors involved knew videoing officers showering was not appropriate, but they did it anyway. The navy's new approach is a step, but not a big enough step.

Phil Geldart shared some ideas with Deb on preventing situations such as the one on the *Wyoming*, and I adapted his idea as a potential solution for the submarine navy. The following scenario is completely doable for a business too:

To prevent another *Wyoming* scenario, I would select two or three chiefs from the boat the female officers were assigned to. I would ask each of the chiefs if they would be willing to sponsor new female officers. You might ask why a lower-ranking enlisted crew member should sponsor an officer. My answer is that the chiefs have street credibility, are hand-picked because they are respected, and have juice because they hold the rank of chief. They are going to be a mentor to the new officer, not a bodyguard. Women who raise their hand to serve on an all-male boat, especially the first women, don't need a body guard; they are tough enough. They need an introduction, support, and access to the street credibility the chiefs can give them to exponentially speed the norming process, so when the chief says a female crew member's got game, she's in the club. Because women have not traditionally served as full-time members of a submarine crew, separate accommodation isn't enough. I would also suggest enlisted women are assigned sponsors/mentors when introduced to the submarine, as officers are upon their introduction. Now that the submarine navy has suffered this blemish on its reputation, it cannot bring onboard women, officers or not, until there's more support.

Be ever vigilant, US Navy.

THE BOTTOM LINE OF INCLUSION

By now you have learned the details of The System. You also understand that the anchors to The System are good communication, healthy conflict, norms, and leadership. These characteristics anchor The System in place. The lack of these anchors contributed to the situation on the USS *Wyoming*. The System hummed along: there was an ombudsman, crew-munity, and all other elements of The System—but without those crucial anchors. You also know that career counselors and qualification officers tie the crew to their personal development and to the mission of the organization. The following is a quick recap of The System's five main steps:

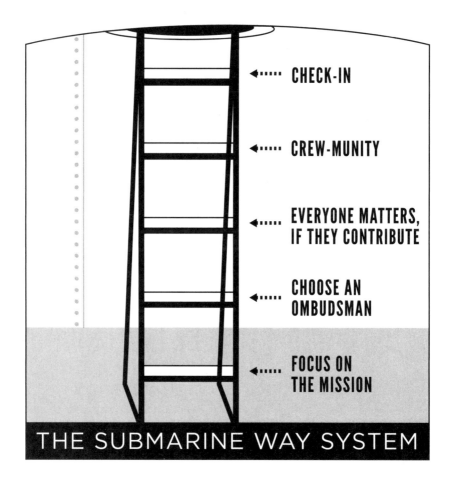

Check-In: The system of onboarding is so robust that upon completion, new crew members (business associates) have everything necessary for the job, including tools, contacts, and familiarity with the environment. They also understand their unique contribution to the success of the mission. They are welcomed in the most practical way, according to their contribution.

Crew-Munity: A healthy blending of a team is necessary to make the individual strengths of the team into a synergistic fighting machine, whether the fight is for revenue, client satisfaction, or fighting the bad guys in the Atlantic Ocean.

Everyone matters, if they contribute: This is the process of identifying the unique contributions of the team members, providing the training to make sure they are successful, and holding them accountable for results. High levels of accountability during and after the training are key.

Choose an Ombudsman: In a submarine, this official liaises with the command and takes the pulse of the crew-munity. In the business world, the ombudsman has direct access to the most senior leaders of the organization. If these individuals do not have authority to drive change, they will not be effective.

Focus on the mission: Focus should be directed to a clear understanding of the goals of the organization overall, as well as individual and organizational daily goals.

In summarizing The System, Gallup's understanding of engagement is relevant. Gallup's Q12 statements all speak to one or more of the systems of inclusion. For example, Q1, "I know what's expected of me at work," is in play from the moment a new crewman steps onboard. The very first system—check-in—ensures that many of the expectations are clear, and qualification makes sure they are all very clear. Add focus to the mission and you have an effective one-two punch in addressing Q1. The Q6 statement, "Someone at work cares about my development," applied to a submarine, means *everyone*, the whole crew-munity, cares. The Q4 statement, "My supervisor or someone at work cares about me as a person," can refer to ombudsmen because of the fact that some supervisors don't properly address employees' needs. Their presence in an organization ensures that someone has the specific responsibility of caring for each worker's welfare, and the anchor role of supervisor, or ombudsmen, also ensures workers' issues are addressed. The Q4 statement implies that teamwork and support, even for personal situations, is beyond compare. While not directly stated in this book, I have mentally mapped all Gallup's Q12 statements to the inclusion systems. Gallup's Q12 Employee Engagement Survey is without a doubt a powerful tool.

Our systems of inclusion directly correlate to engagement. A massive benefit of the inclusion systems is that they raise engagement, producing the benefits of a highly engaged workforce. When I served with the navy, there were no surveys to measure engagement on a submarine, but we were without a doubt engaged. It was completely measurable through successful mission after successful mission.

Inclusion happened over and over, from submarine to submarine. From my experience, I suspect an organization using The System might double its level of engagement if it is currently at the US business average of 32 percent (the percentage reported in Gallup's 2016 *Q12 Meta-Analysis* report.) From our combined experience in business, neither Deb nor I is aware of a process or system that directly maps to engagement and can specifically improve engagement, but we both believe The System does.

We conclude with statistics taken from Gallup's 2016 *Q12 Meta-Analysis* report.

THE ROI OF INCLUSION THROUGH ENGAGEMENT

- ☑ A highly engaged organization, as compared to a poorly engaged organization, has 17 percent higher productivity.

- ☑ Highly engaged organizations also deliver 22 percent higher profitability.

- ☑ Highly engaged organizations have 20 percent higher sales.

- ☑ Highly engaged organizations have 43 percent lower absenteeism.

- ☑ Highly engaged organizations have 70 percent fewer safety incidents.

- ☑ Highly engaged organizations have 52 percent lower employee turnover. Lost employees cost organizations one to three times their annual wages, with this number higher for senior people.

- ☑ Highly engaged health-care organizations have 58 percent fewer patient safety incidences.

THE ROI OF CONTINUOUS TRAINING AS IT LEADS TO IMPROVED INCLUSION

- ☑ One popular restaurant invests $2,000 annually per employee in employee training. This chain makes $1,000 per square foot of space, double the industry average.

- ☑ A well-known business process outsourcing (BPO) company conducted training for managing virtual teams and experienced a 7 percent growth in sales.[4]

---

4   LearnCore, December 8, 2014.

It isn't an accident that focus on continuous growth helps to drive inclusion on submarines.

ROI OF DIVERSITY AND INCLUSION:

☑ Eighty-four percent of executives surveyed in a March 2015 Korn Ferry study reported that a lack of attention to inclusion causes employee turnover.

☑ New data from the **Peterson Institute for International Economics** and **Ernst & Young** bolsters the case for inclusion. **Results from 21,980 global, publicly traded companies** in various industries and sectors in ninety-one countries showed that having at least 30 percent of women in leadership positions adds 6 percent to the net profit margin.

Although powerful, none of this information takes into consideration the cost of litigation resulting from inclusion and diversity suits, or the impact on recruiting when your organization gets a bad rap for diversity and inclusion issues. If there is a system to ensure you are including everyone, doesn't it make sense to use it?

OUR SERVICES

Deb is founder and president and John is keynote speaker and advisor at The Submarine Way. The company offers keynote speaking, consulting, coaching, and training on The Submarine Way. Training is experiential, meaning the student experiences the feel of a submarine environment. The instructor wears a poopy suit, and a Klaxon alarm wails to open the session. Students walk away with a physical and mental experience of what it takes for inclusion to stick.

Contact us through **thesubmarineway@gmail.com,** or through the website at **www.thesubmarineway.com.**